Dedicated to the Familial Loves in My Life...

Elizabeth Ann Springsteen Crawford*, my beloved mother, who, by her demeanor and actions, taught me to forgive, to let go and let God, advised me to do what's right, and showed me how to love unconditionally. Because of those lessons learned, my heart is forever happy, light, and free.*

Thomas Louis Crawford*, my beloved father, who was and is always here for me in every way needed and possible. You set the bar high for parental commitment and responsibility. Because of your example, I will always live honestly and challenge with integrity.*

Dr. Charlene Alice Crawford Peterson*, my beloved sister, who I am blessed and proud to know as a doctor now, and who will always be my big sister "Chy," loving me, looking out for me, encouraging and proud of me. I am very thankful for you.*

Hunter "One" Nathanael Smith*, my beloved first-born son, who reminded me that being open, welcoming, and forthright, and following your heart and dreams are the optimal ways to exist.*

Garland "G-man" Thomas-Emmanuel Smith*, my beloved second-born son, who showed me that patience and understanding lead to peace of mind and that the "you do you" lifestyle is the ultimate way of living!*

I love you ***ALL*** *forever!*

Give Take Be

Carol Crawford Smith

ISBN: 1515238903
ISBN 13: 9781515238904

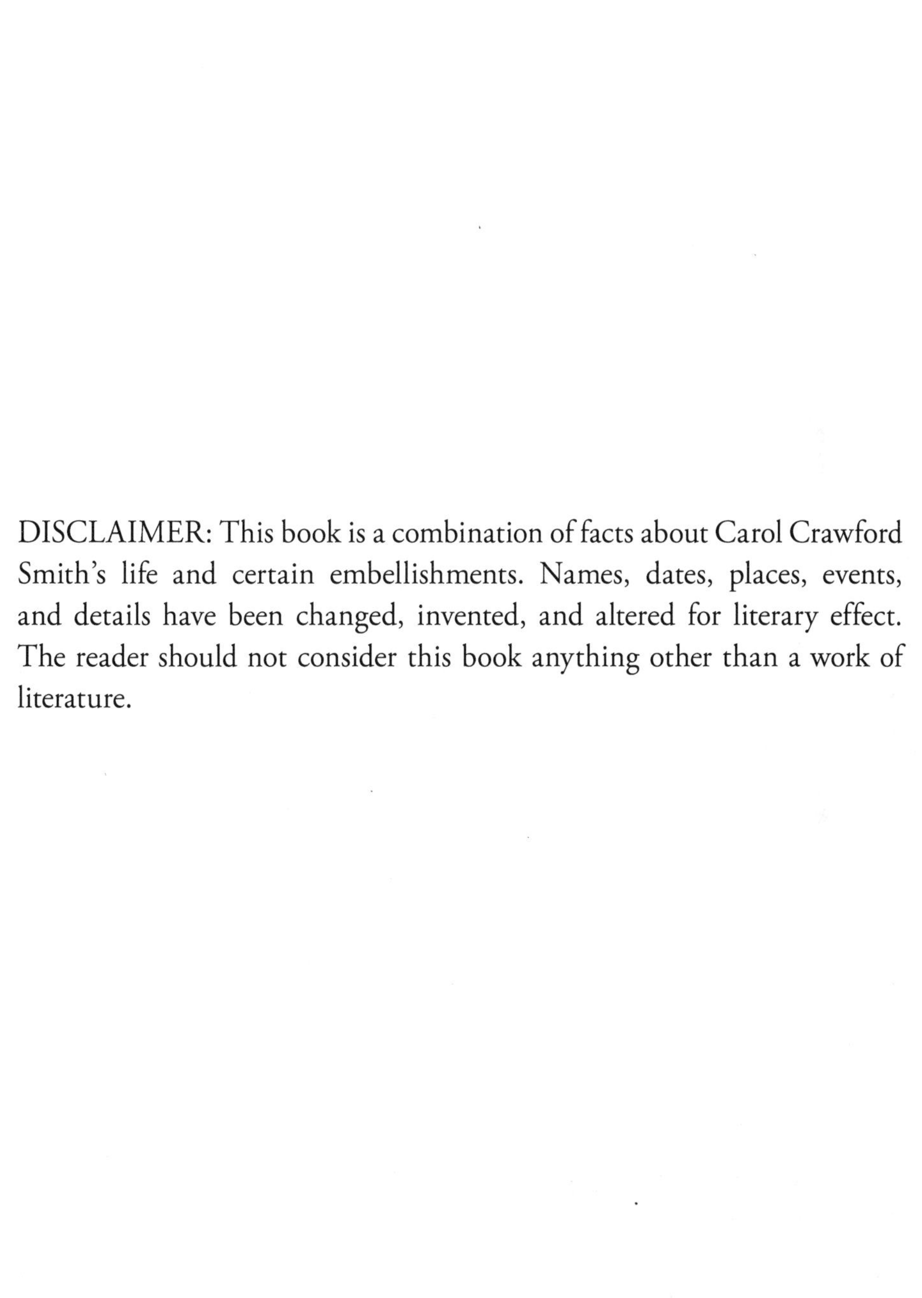

DISCLAIMER: This book is a combination of facts about Carol Crawford Smith's life and certain embellishments. Names, dates, places, events, and details have been changed, invented, and altered for literary effect. The reader should not consider this book anything other than a work of literature.

Table of Contents (Program)

A Quote and Author Statement...

"So how do you measure LOVE? I measure LOVE every day! I thank God I have been given another day to see the sun and all his creation. You can feel love from miles away. You can taste love in every bite of food. You can hear love in a song or a baby's laughter. You can smell love in a flower! Love is everywhere, so it exists ... you just have to use your measuring sticks....your senses!"

—Marshall Johnson, Jr., Filmmaker

My friend, Marshall, wrote the previous prose, reminding me what love is. Upon reading it, a fire ignited in me to get this thing done. "What thing?" you may ask. Well, the thing is the book of a life! It's the life story of an extraordinary person who lived to find brightness in every day through dance, love, family, and God. I am here now with the talent, ability, passion, and desire to do what I am called to do out of love, so, I write. Life is worth living when you do what you love. My love is twofold. As a human development practitioner, I also love helping people actualize their goals and dreams, and I endeavor to do so in this relatable account of my life experiences.

—The Author

Introduction

Carol Crawford Smith is formerly a professional ballet dancer with Dance Theatre of Harlem (1978–1988). Carol founded The Center of Dance in Blacksburg, Virginia in 1994 to share and provide excellence in her beloved art form with students and enthusiasts in the community and beyond. A diagnosis of multiple sclerosis in year 2000 and subsequent rapid physical debilitation halted her ability to dance and threatened to end her career as a dance teacher.

In stepped ABC. In December of 2005, after a lengthy and suspenseful application process, the network, by way of *Extreme Makeover: Home Edition* (Lock and Key Productions), awarded Carol Crawford Smith a dream home and state of the art dance business, enabling her to live and work accessibly. When the show first aired on February 12, 2006, twenty-three million viewers watched Carol and her sons receive the new home and remodeled dance studio. In the years since, millions more have viewed the inspirational story of the Smith Family as the show aired in syndication on cable channels, including TV Land, Lifetime, and The Country Network in the United States, as well as, on many other television stations worldwide. Today, Carol continues to teach and produce dance events and is a published writer of magazine columns and books that motivate and inspire readers to achieve greatness beyond their imaginations.

Give Take Be is a memoir of Carol Crawford Smith presented as a theatrically themed piece of literary art. Throughout the triumphs and trials of love, family, and dis-ease, Carol undertakes a journey of self-actualization, maintaining a good heart and beautiful spirit while experiencing relationships and situations that could either uplift or destroy.

Carol is a dancer, but this story is not about dance. It is an opportunity to enjoy scenarios and find power through sympathy and understanding to dance on with the phenomena of living life! It has been said that "life is a stage." If that is the case, the curtain is now open on the life of Carol Crawford Smith.

A Letter...

My Dear Girlfriend,

I write with hope that this letter finds you well. You know that book I was working on called *Give Take Be*? Well, after I finished it a couple of months ago, I believed a bestseller masterpiece had been created. I poured my heart and soul into the writing, disclosing a lot of secrets, and releasing a great deal of anger and grief. Though I chose to present it as someone else's story, everyone, who read it and knows me, and even those who read it and only know of me, gathered that it was my story, though I insisted it was about the life of a fictitious character named Suzanne Baptiste.

The writing is believable and engaging. One friend who I invited to read the manuscript said she could not put it down once she began reading. She said she read with great anticipation of what would happen next, and even reached for the tissues a number of times when reading the 'Scene' called "Bennett" about a past love affair. Her enthusiasm assured me that I had created something good. She said it was worth going the full distance to have it published, and that I should contact ever person I know who is well-connected and who could lead me to getting the work published through a major publisher. She was brutally honest upon reading it, and admonished me for not presenting it as my story. Needless to say, her encouragement left me feeling hopeful and evermore proud.

I also shared it with a fellow writer, Alexis Wilson, who self-published her first book *Not So Black and White*, a few years ago. She graciously took the time to read it, provided editorial comments and gave feedback on the third self-edited version of the book. She, too, thought my book was well done and applauded my "voice." Her review came first, actually, and left me feeling hopeful of literary success. I know she equated the writing to my story because she asked for clarity on personal parts, and suggested I write with more sensitivity regarding issues pertaining to "your son." She went on to say my writing made her wish she had been more colorful and revealing about experiences with her lovers.

My mother read about two-thirds of the initial manuscript. It was too close to home for her and too much "true confessions," as she described it. She said much of what was written should be left between me and God and that it was no one else's business. Deep down I know mother knows best, though I carried on like I know more than her. I told her to stop reading it if she could not disassociate the writing from my—essentially, our life. I know better now, after having talked to her, that it is not my place nor right to disclose family matters under the guise of fiction, no matter how hurt or angry or justified I was feeling at the time of writing.

The big kick came after my highly prominent literary friend, Nikki Giovanni, read some of the manuscript while on an overseas trip, and made a special visit to me at my home to share her opinion. I spent hours prior to her visit imaging the accolades and praise she would give and the leads to agents and publishers she would provide. I was sure all financial worries would soon be a thing of the past, as the connections she would make would result in a multi-million-dollar contract with a ten percent or hundreds-of-thousands-of-dollars advance from a major publishing house.

Nikki visited me at my home on a Tuesday. We were very happy to see each other and immediately shared profound stories and updates about summer adventures. All the while, the anticipation of favorable comments from her on my book bubbled within me. When the niceties were behind us, she sat down adjacent to me at the dining room table, put down her copy of the book and said, "You've got a problem, here." I smiled, my bubble still fully inflated, thinking I had misheard or misunderstood her. As the conversation continued, I migrated to a daze of acceptance of her opinion that pricked at my slowly deflating ego. "Who cares about Vincent?" she asked, and continued, "I had to stop reading. No one cares to know about Vincent." When I stopped nodding in agreement and saw clearly enough to look past my disappointment, I heard her say the book should be about me. I heard her say I had a wonderful story about being a professional dancer stricken with a debilitating disease that people would want to read. I heard her say people will seek to see themselves through my story and gain inspiration. She also said I should write like I was having a conversation with my girlfriend.

Months later, Nikki sent me a copy of *brown girl, dreaming*, by Jacqueline Woodson, as an example of a poetic verse style of writing an autobiography. I love the book and the chance to experience Woodson's life through her words and format, and her approach registers to me as being absolutely perfect for her. I do not think I could write my story truly and completely for me, in the style Woodson presents her life. Storytelling is a love and a strength that I can most comfortably do in narrative form. Painting pictures with words as a narrated story is what I do well. The artist, that is me, brings words to life naturally with vibrant rhythm and flow, just as the dancer I was born to be, instinctively knows how to move her body and experience every undulation on a cellular level. I write, articulating my thoughts for the reader to sense my words completely. All said, after reading and processing Woodson's work, I know I could learn how to write in verse form, but for *Give Take Be* it is narrative prose.

So, I returned to the drawing board day after day, week after week, month after month reading, dissecting, deleting, editing, writing and re-writing what I, originally presented as finished. The comments and responses from everyone who read the first and earlier drafts, whether all or in part, were ALL taken into consideration, as well as, incorporated to some degree. In the end, *Give Take Be* is now about me, and it is my story. It is a memoir of experiences in my life presented theatrically. This colorful, artistic autobiography of love and life is presented in acts and scenes because I know and relate to dance, theater, and the stage, so completely, and I want the reader to relate to that side of me. As you read, imagine each "Act" opening and closing with a curtain, and save your review (applause) for the end.

I hope you enjoy this book (show) with a loving and open heart, as was mine when it was written (performed).

Yours forever, Love,
Carol

P. S. Vincent is now played by Aaron.

Preface

THE PHRASE "GIVE TAKE BE" was introduced to me by a man affectionately known as Mr. Bill. There are at least fifty people in this world who can relate to the instruction, for together, as members of Dance Theatre of Harlem, we observed and learned first-hand from the man. William Griffith was my ballet teacher. He believed in me as a young dance artist, and that greatly nourished my sense of self-worth. When I took care to coordinate my leotard, tights, legwarmers and other accessories, dolled-up my hair and wore light make-up on top of that, he took note and complimented me. He would often compare me to Prima Ballerina Lynn Seymour, who he had once taught and coached. His compliments and comparisons made my day. I grabbed those positive thoughts, imbedded them in my memory, and draw upon their essence to this day as I travel gracefully through the journey of my life.

Give Take Be is a catchy, engaging, and intriguing title. Like the title I submitted to a cousin who invited me to name a work of art he created. The image in his piece is of a book being held. Behind the book is a figure presumed to be reading. Splattered between the book and the figure is red, painted like blood exploding from the head of the person reading. I submitted the title *Blood Read (Read pronounced reed or red. You decide.)* My case for this title is that it is intriguing yet engaging and provides the opportunity to explore the depths of the image and decide the title that best fits, thus drawing viewers into the art and encouraging a deeper connection to the work. Whether or not the reader will feel more connected to this writing because of the catchy, engaging, and intriguing title is unknown, but I hope this is the case.

My long-time student and dear friend, writer Ann Goette, who publishes under the name Ann Goethe, suggested that *Give Take Be* would make an excellent title for the book I had mentioned I wanted to write. She had heard me use the phrase repeatedly over the past 20-plus years that she had been studying ballet with me. The instruction accompanies a specific *port de bras*, or movement of the arms ending combinations when the final arm position is rounded overhead in a position called high fifth. The arm opens to what is known as second position, as if to present it or "Give"; then the arm lowers and gathers to round and meet the barre arm in low fifth with head inclining towards the barre to "Take"; from there, the head turns away from the barre as subtly or as dramatically as instructed to finish the combination and simply "Be." The observer or teacher of the action is the one to interpret the routine when done. "Is the student convincing and confident?" "Did the arms and head transition in a smooth coordinated *epaulmente* (positioning of the head and shoulders)?" These are the affects a dancer works to achieve and perfect, and a dance teacher is skilled to interpret and evaluate. Here, I am the writer creating the script, and you are the reader or observer entrusted with determining if the writing flows smoothly, is coordinated, makes sense, and is convincing. Also, this platform of prose provides, or gives, you the opportunity to read it, and thus take it in and decide if it is successful. The determination then leaves us both to simply be and move onto where ever the creative winds of curiosity direct and flow.

Carol Crawford Smith

Prologue

I HOLD MY CHEST HIGH and my chin up every day with confidence, conviction and courage, voyaging through life as a mother, dancer, lover and daughter. My name is Carol Crawford Smith. I am a class act. But who am I, really? I am the product, the mix of all things good. I am the crème de la crème cocoa-chocolate brown, Monterey Jack, cheddar and brie cheese aged to perfection, muscle-toned thick and beefy fondue that's been pulled, melted, stretched, swirled, flipped, and twisted with a half-life of fifty-one years behind me and, prayerfully, the same ahead. I am yummy and delicious! Everyone wants a taste of me. Yet, there are many more layers and levels in the answer of that question. This book reveals them and leaves to digest them. Moving beyond the ego-tripping, I will sum up aspects of the answer in a commencement speech given to the Blacksburg (Virginia) High School graduating class of 2004 with parents, teachers, families, and friends in attendance...

Be a Class Act

I am a dancer, a teacher of dance, and the owner of a dance studio. A few months ago, a sealed envelope was handed to me after teaching a class. The deliverer was one of my long-time students and friends. She was very enthusiastic and excited about me reading what was inside the envelope. Truthfully, I was not. I had so much on my mind.

First of all, I wasn't feeling the greatest and had a terrible headache. I was tired and just wanted to go home and spend a relaxed evening with my sons. It wasn't until the following day that I opened the envelope. My mind was clearer, and I was in a better place to consider the news or task that requested my attention.

"Dear Ms. Crawford Smith," the letter began. It continued to state compliments and accolades about my persona and the contribution I have made to the community. The letter continued, "… you are a source of artistic and professional vibrancy, you possess many wonderful qualities that are admired by all. We would be privileged and elated if you would act as commencement speaker for our graduation ceremony," end quote. Well, what is the date, folks? It's obvious what my response was. I was so honored and felt so appreciated. I felt like jumping for joy and crying at the same time. Then it occurred to me. I have been asked to provide one of the greatest honors for the graduating class this year. I have been asked to send you budding scholars and leaders of our future off with words of wisdom! In doing so, I would have to incorporate details of personal experience to motivate you to achieve great feats in life. I am expected to share my deepest, darkest secrets in hopes that you graduating seniors and the viewing audience will receive the true message of my address and not leave with frivolous and juicy gossip about Carol Crawford Smith.

Well, everything I do is a class act, and I intend for this commencement address to fit within that category. Mostly, I intend to leave you with the message to be a class act in whatever you do.

Being a class act was instilled in me at a young age. What I've come to realize is that being a class act means nothing if you cannot be honest, if you cannot be yourself, and if you cannot act with your best interest at heart without forsaking that of others. I am a mother of two boys ages 10 and 8. Like many parents, I claim to know what is best for my children. The qualifiers are that I have been there, and in many cases, still am, and prefer that my children not encounter the hard knocks known to exist out there. If any of you parents, share my sentiments, I suggest it may be time to get over it. Ups and downs are a part of life—as cliché as it may sound. Let your children go, and trust they will be OK.

This is a glorious day … a day of celebration … a day when parents and loved ones can be proud of the accomplishment that a baby … born sometime in the mid 1980's … is achieving today. The baby is graduating from preparatory education and venturing into the world. Some of you may have already journeyed on the path that extends into adulthood. You may have applied and been accepted to college. You may plan to move to, or visit, another geographical area to study a new language and culture. Or, you may plan to remain close to home to work and earn money to help fund your eventual continued education. And, there are those who will take no immediate action and simply contemplate the options before making a decision about what's next. The scenarios, whether ideal or unreal, are as varied and numerous as there are the number of you in this graduating class.

I speak from common sense and experience. My scenario at graduating from high school began at age fourteen. Still in high school and a rising tenth grader, I was invited to join the internationally acclaimed ballet company Dance Theatre of Harlem. How exciting and somewhat unbelievable that was when you consider I began a serious study of ballet only six years prior. Without hesitation and with the support and encouragement of my parents, I joined the dance arts organization. Within months, and throughout the next decade, I was in rehearsals with the who's who of the dance world elite … George Balanchine, founder of New York City Ballet … Alexandra Danilova, former ballerina assoluta of the historic Ballet Russe de Monte Carlos … Agnes DeMilles, dancer, choreographer, writer, and kin to Hollywood royalty Cecil B. DeMilles … Jerome Robbins, famed choreographer of musical hits West Side Story *and* On the Town … *Tennessee Williams, who was consulted by Valerie Beattis on the creation of her ballet version of* A Streetcar Named Desire.

What may sound like a fantasy world to others was normal existence for this at-one-time-wet-behind-the-ears teenager. As normal, was the fact that I had to complete my high school education while touring internationally and performing and rehearsing forty weeks out of the fifty-two weeks per calendar year, AND I had to complete it with no less than honors. You see, the directors, Arthur Mitchell and Karel Shook required those of us who were still in school to maintain grades of B+ or above or we were let go and sent back home. Thusly motivated, I graduated from high school with honors, ultimately became a principal soloist, and achieved a ten-year career with the acclaimed dance company. Being accepted into Dance Theatre of Harlem in 1978 was a great feat! But, what else could be expected? I am an exceptional dancer, and many years ago, a dance sovereign recognized it. Now, I teach my students to be the best in dance, as well as, in whatever else they choose to do in life. Naturally, a version of this expectation also applies to my children.

A few handfuls of you have graced the sprung floors of my studio. So, I can rightfully call you my students. But today, I consider all of you to be my students. We share a common space today, and I have been selected … if only for a brief moment … to share and teach knowledge and insight on what it takes to be the best in life … to be a class act.

It is not uncommon for me to teach and/or leave a message no matter where I go, no matter what I do, or to whomever I speak. As a child, I realized my gift to be a teacher … a motivator … a mentor. Though I have lived up to the expectation much of my adult life, I truthfully enjoy being a student first.

The joy of learning recently brought me back to school. In December of 2003, after eighteen months of dedicated study, I received a Master of Science degree in Human Development. I was one of nine in the inaugural class of the Human Development master's program. My parents accompanied me as I walked across the stage in Cassell Coliseum to receive the diploma folder and shake the hand of the university president. I literally required my father's hand and solid frame to walk those near thirty feet because the walk was challenging. Symbolically, my parents have been holding my hand and helping me walk paths and have experiences throughout my lifetime. In fact, they are here today to see me achieve yet one more accomplishment. Their support keeps me strong.

If it's not your mother and father who helped you to get here, several some ones had your best interest at heart for the past seventeen or so years. People cared for you, nurtured, mentored and encouraged you to make it to these seats of honor. Mothers and fathers, thank you. Thank you for the diaper changing, the burped stained tee shirts bleached white again, the scraped knees medicated and bandaged, the transportation to soccer games and ballet lessons, not to mention the resources spent to enable participation in these activities. Thank you for the cars, which were absolutely required because it is not cool to ride the school bus once you are in the twelfth grade, and for the resources yet to be applied to future ventures such as tuition for college, dresses and receptions for weddings, new apartments and homes for a start in life. Oh, and did I thank you for extra dips in the coffers for gas so the vehicles can run? Parents, guardians, and relatives, I am not trying to dampen anyone's mood by mentioning the seemingly endless supply of funds you may still have to provide for your child. The intention is to give credit and pay tribute to the ones who helped these seniors get to where they are today.

Students, gratitude is also due to your teachers. Teachers and other school personnel are part of the glue that held you together. They knew when you were struggling academically and challenged you to strive for better. They gave you failing grades when it was unavoidable and praised your accomplishments when it was undeniable. Your teachers heard your concerns and showed empathy when you felt you could not go to your parents for belief that they would not understand. Parents, if your child turns to others, it is not because you were not doing a good job. A child calling upon a secondary agent is an assuring reminder that the support network extends beyond the homestead walls. Students, it's common for teachers and parents to be allies in defense for your present with the intention to ensure a bright future. In the past ten years of running a dance business, students of all ages have been under my artistic tutelage. Parents of children in elementary school to college age have called me to talk privately about concerns for their child, asking what I may have observed and what I can do to help. I do not hesitate to offer my observations and insights into any perceived situation. If it is an obvious self-esteem issue, I am in the position to build up the child genuinely and sincerely by acknowledging their technical achievement. Acknowledgement occurs through awarding a deserved role in the end-of-the-year production or assigning a position of leadership as an instructor or instructor's assistant.

Students, I am sure your teachers have done similarly. I experience relative occurrences in a local elementary school where the "senior" class of fifth graders are assigned jobs, such as peer mediators, safety patrols, kindergarten helpers, and PE assistants. These roles are tremendous esteem builders. The students are awarded a sense of responsibility and shown that the adults have confidence in them to do a job well. My son was a morning announcer. (Said with humor; I am convinced he was assigned the position because he had his mother's undeniably good DNA for command in public speaking and has the genetic ability to confidently present before an attentive audience.) He never missed a day of duty. And, he was never late for his job. In fact, he insisted on riding the school bus on the days he was to speak to ensure being at school in plenty of time before announcements were scheduled to begin.

Four of our graduating seniors have been called upon to provide leadership at my studio. They are reliable and dependable young ladies.

They have taught classes, rehearsed children for performance, learned and perfected choreography in which they were cast, and built costumes for admiring young dancers. I take partial credit for their leadership development. After all, I exercised my decision-making authority and offered them their well-deserved roles. They accepted and maintained their duty, and often challenged me to allow them more freedom and autonomy in the execution of their job. I respect them because they take initiative and express confidence in their abilities while showing respect and a willingness to learn from people who are more experienced and capable.

This is one opinionated description of these young ladies. I may be right to comment similarly about all of the graduating seniors. Traits of achievement, dedication, commitment, and accomplishment are inherent in all of you. You would not be where you are today, if such were not imbedded. And, you would not be where you are today if it weren't for the unlimited individuals who boosted you up and gave you a springboard from which to take off.

This brings us to the next category of people to thank. You are justified to thank each other, your classmates. Look at the person beside you … Look at the person to the left and to the right … Now, see the person in front of you and the person behind … And, see the person way over on the opposite side of the commencement congregation. (Go ahead. I am going to take a moment for you to do just that.) In doing so, send a message of love and well wishes. Send it to every one whose eyes you make contact with as well as to the one who just crosses your mind. Send it to the one who was ignored and ridiculed throughout the year, or throughout their high school career. Send it to the one you went to the prom with, the one who helped you pick out your prom dress, as well as, to the one who wore the same prom dress, but in a different color. Send it to the one whose action made you feel humiliated when he or she stole your boyfriend or girlfriend. You may want to send extra love and gratitude in that case, because you probably did not need to be in a relationship with that person in the first place. Send it to the one who may be differently able then you. You can help with what that person may be challenged to do at this moment. You may need to call on that person one day, and chances are he or she will be there for you.

The bonds you have built and the experiences you have had with one another will, to some degree, carry on for the rest of your life. You will remember the late night study sessions with cohorts of a chemistry class. You will remember the friend who made you think twice about drinking at a party because you were not of age AND because you had to drive home afterwards. In more ways than time permits or are appropriate to mention here, I would not doubt you have been one another's lifesaver and confidante when the chips were down. Maintain the productive and supportive relationships you have built. Maintain them for the rest of your life. And, for the relationships that do not quite fit, or have yet to fit in those categories, again I encourage you to send thoughts of love and accolades to all. I am a firm believer that love sent will come back to you tenfold in beyond imaginable and extremely welcomed ways.

Graduating Class, I have accepted and achieved the task you presented to me … the task to be your commencement speaker. It has been an honor and a privilege, and I thank YOU. Now, I have a task or final assignment for you. It is an assignment I hope you will work on endlessly. There is another generation of future graduates out in the audience today. You are their heroes. They see you up here beautifully adorned and handsomely clad in cap and gown, awaiting the ceremonious walk across the stage to receive a well-deserved high school diploma. In whatever you choose to do … be a class act. They are watching, your support network is behind you, and I hope for your greatest success!

I closed the commencement address with sincere blessings and heartfelt congratulations, and I chose this commencement speech to open a disclosure of my life, what I do, and what I have done which, as I see it, is synonymous with Give Take Be. As a mother I do unconditionally and endlessly sacrifice for my children (Give). I am a true and honest person who indiscriminately and fairly evaluates the facts of all situations called to my attention to determine and decide what, if any, is the best course of action (Take). I am a lover who has been loved intensely and who has loved deeply and dearly. As a youth, I learned what it feels like to love another person outside of my family. As an adult, I learned from another how to be loved only to eventually know yet another love who gave me the greatest loves of my life, my children. Intertwined within this amorous existence is my life-sustaining love for dance that shapes how I walk, how I talk, to whom I talk, and why. Mother, love, and dance are the trinity of ingredients that, when mixed together with uncompromising poise and presence, formulate the one and only me (Be).

ACT 1

Lessons in Love

SCENE 1

Through the Classroom Window

"Forty-three years ago, he saw me through the classroom window and knew I was the one."

THIS IS A REMARKABLE TIME in my life. It is the beginning of the rest of my amazing life, and I finally know how to live it with great joy and happiness. I live it with the man made just for me. He pumps lotion and rubs my tired legs daily. He kisses the frontal lobe of my forehead and the nape of my neck, moving unhurriedly from either location to my ear to nibble and whisper sensual, healing words that sooth my yearning heart and ignite my sleeping body. We are together in my imagination. The vision of us occurs in my dreams. Now more than ever I want it to be reality, but it cannot. Forty-three years ago, he saw me through the classroom window and knew I was the one. I did not see him then nor recognize our kindred spirit, but I know it now. Some people have a love that is timeless—a love that lasts throughout eternity. Our love is that, though we never married nor consummated. We did not need to do such acts for our love to exist endlessly in the spirit, in our dreams, though we existed in the flesh. We were definitely made for each other. I know this in my heart as sure as I know our love was divinely ordained.

We kissed tenderly and short upon saying goodbye the last time we were together. The kiss was no more than a prolonged touch of lips, and as innocent as a goodbye kiss on the cheek. I sat satisfied and dazed after he left, still feeling the softness of his plump lips touching mine. That one tender touch from him was all I needed to bring on a flood of memories and thoughts of how wonderful we were together. I walked that day in the city. I walked down the steps he had carried me up three fourths of an hour earlier. He was not as strong as he appeared, or used to be. He struggled and rested mid-way up. My manila-brown burly bear was older and, though massive in size, he was soft, with a round belly and diminished, flabby bottom. He was not in the best of shape. He was determined to carry me up those stairs, however, so he could hold me, feel me, and, so I could see what was at the top. I loved him for that.

The wheelchair was waiting for me at the landing top. I sat in it with his assistance. He pushed me. We rolled into my friends Michaela and Terence's bedroom, where the rooftop door was open—I was on vacation, visiting my friends. It was a bright, sunny, hot and humid day in July on which an infrequent summer breeze streamed inside, not to lend comfort but to take your breath away. After rolling me into the room, Aaron sat on the steps leading out the open door to catch a whiff of humidity. I remained in the chair so we could face each other, positioned just right to capture any residual air that squeezed past his large frame. Though it had been three years since I'd last seen him and thirty before that, our demeanor was comfortable and familiar. It hardly felt like we had been apart. I wanted the time together to last forever. We should be talking about what we would have for dinner and which movie to watch that night before going to bed. Such conversation was forbidden, however, and he would leave in less than an hour. To make the most of our time together, a nearby bottle of lotion became my ploy to bring us closer without crossing the line.

"I am a bit dry" I said while pumping lotion into my left hand. "My legs are tired and ashy, too. Could you lotion and rub them?" I motioned him towards the bottle pump while distributing lavender-scented lotion between my hands.

Okay." He reached and pumped. I pulled my pants up to the knees to reveal my cocoa-brown dancer-calves and shins that I'd gracefully sculpted over decades in marley-covered sprung-floored dance studios. Remarkably, they remained gorgeous. I had not so much as walked in six years, let alone danced, but there I sat, exposing them, in anticipation of his soothing touch and lotion massage.

As he rubbed my legs, we looked at one another and talked of the ordinary and mundane. "So how far is the medical center from here?" I asked. It was a simple, safe question, but what I really wanted to know was if he still loved me. The inquiry would have been rhetorical. I knew he loved me still and certainly loved the idea of us. I knew because he had told me many times since we reconnected. I knew it for the very reason he left his hospital job at the state penitentiary and drove to New York to see me. For a couple of short hours, I would have Aaron Waters, R. N., caring for me, just as it should be.

Terence was out on the roof smoking. Michaela did not allow him to smoke inside, so he found refuge in a cigarette up two stairs and out the door, on the exterior side of their bedroom wall, while Aaron and I were in their bedroom during the lotion rub. Terence was talking on his cell between and during cigarette draws and puffs. His demeanor suggested he was minding his own business, but his position was within earshot of Aaron and me. Though a comfort to be around, Terence was a frightening, yet, somewhat fascinating sight to see. He was a short and scrawny, dual-complexion chain-smoking, retired fisherman with a shaggy goatee, which he intentionally kept long and untamed in deliberate contrast to the absent follicles on his vitiligo-spotted scalp. A fishing accident had left him with prostheses from his left wrist to what were once the tips of his fingers. I had little doubt the dis-membered fisherman was eavesdropping out on the rooftop. It did not matter if he heard us, though. Aaron and I were not saying anything incriminating.

Aaron rubbed lotion on my calves, shins, and ankles with the love, care and patience a new parent would have for a child just born. He gently soothed, glided and touched me with each application. I could have easily closed my eyes and drifted away with a "Luther" melody repeatedly playing in my mind; "It's alright, it's alright, it's alright. It's alright, it's alright. It's alright." It felt so perfect, so right, so real. It was real! It was really happening. For a while, which seemed forevermore, I was in eternal peace with the man made for me. The beauty of our inside-off-the-rooftop relating would soon come to an abrupt and undesirable end. Aaron stopped rubbing my legs and wiped his hands. "I got to go," he said, seemingly no longer smitten in my fantasy—or, his care—of soothing me, but sounding mindful of his responsibilities to his household and self.

The graveyard shift had Aaron living nocturnally. Checking in at the hospital at midnight and off duty at eight o'clock meant going to bed by two o'clock in the afternoon for a decent 'nights' rest. He would be up at ten o'clock and out the door by eleven to drive to work, just to punch the clock at midnight and do it all over again. Though needing to leave, Aaron unhurriedly stood after placing my pants' legs down and carefully rolled me out of the bedroom to the top of the stairs. I had strength in my legs and flexibility enough to take steps, so he held me under my armpits from behind and boosted me up to stand. He was determined that I walk down the stairs, as determined as he had been forty minutes earlier to carry me up, and for the same reason: he wanted to hold me.

Upon leaving the bedroom, we had called to our host. At hearing and seeing us leave, Terence came in from the rooftop and followed us out. As Aaron helped me stand, Terence maneuvered to a position on the first step down in front of me, holding out his arms for me to grasp at the elbows. I leaned to grab him with Aaron now holding me from behind at the waist. To descend, I had to lift from one hip at a time, searching for a sense of the respective hamstrings and quadriceps while balancing feebly on the opposite leg. After alternating the action six times, with the help of Aaron and Terence, I made it to the first landing, where began the last set of stairs down. I was exhausted and asked to sit. While holding my hips, Aaron lowered me to sit between his legs, as he plopped down straddling me. Not only did he get to feel and hold me a lot that day, but he managed to snuggle and 'accidently' slap-brush my fanny by that time in the traverse—like a kid who is dared to run past and slap the behind of a girl at her sixth grade locker. Terence took the rest stop as an opportunity to run back up and get the foldable wheelchair. Aaron had wrapped his arms around my waist by then and embraced me while we were sitting. I folded my arms over his to secure the hold.

Terence left the wheelchair open and in place for me at the bottom of the stairs, then he went onto the first floor balcony for a smoke. Aaron and I stayed put and talked. "I am so happy you came to see me," I said, turning and cocking my head as far right as possible to see him behind me."

"I am so happy to see you, Carol. You look and feel great." He said this with his characteristic hearty chuckle.

"Thank you, Aaron," I ingratiatingly responded with a nod and smile. I knew I looked youthful and, to add to my ageless vibrancy, I had a sprite-like attitude and wrinkle-free face when smiling. It was comfortable talking up-close, looking at Aaron nearly dead-square in the eyes. "We must see each other, again, soon," I insisted, not wanting another three and thirty years to pass before we'd be in each other's presence again.

"We will, as soon as possible," he promised, then pulled his legs up and slung them beside me to gain firm footing to help me stand.

Terence was still outside smoking, and on the phone, once again, so Aaron escorted me solo down the remaining stairs. Before I sat in the chair, Aaron made a move to have one last good hold. He stood directly before me, wrapped his arms around my waist, and pulled me close to him. I wrapped my arms around his neck to stand as tall and as strong as possible. My 5' 5 ½", 115 pounds, lean and toned petite stature metaphorically aligned and fit his 6' 2" robust build as perfectly as a wingless larva securely nestled and encompassed in a nurturing cocoon. We kissed. At that endearing moment of care and strength, thoughts and feelings of physical discomfort were no more. I felt safe and able to elevate and take flight for a moment, and did so in my imagination. Aaron let go and helped me sit, then Terence came in from the balcony as if on cue. Aaron said goodbye, and he and Terence walked out. I sat dream-like, contemplating the touch of his lips on my lips, our holds, and the fantasy of us that came with it. Aaron told me later that, when leaving, he and Terence talked about their mutual passion for fishing and how he'd been in love with me since he first laid eyes on me in elementary school.

Onset of Timeless Love

"All I ever wanted to do from the moment I first laid eyes on you was to marry you." Aaron told me when he called days after saying goodbye on that "lotion-rub, a-time-to-hold" afternoon. He reminisced back to third grade when, he had seen me for the first time through the classroom door's window. "I'd ask to go to the bathroom all of the time just to walk past your classroom door and look at you. My teacher thought I had some sort of bladder problem. The only issue responsible for my frequent bathroom breaks was that I longed for you." When he told me that, I could picture him rising to the balls of his feet to peer at me through that window. I imagined what he felt when seeing me back then and how disappointed he must have been to encounter my obliviousness, bordering disenchantment, bordering disgust that I showed for him all of the time. I must not have been totally insensitive, though, because it was around that time, when we were eight years young, that his mother suddenly died of a brain aneurism. He reminded me of how compassionate I was to him then and how I was the one who got him through that tragic time. "Do you remember what you did?" he asked. "You assured me it would be alright and that I was strong enough to make it through. Those were the words that really helped me because when my mother died, I just wanted to die, too." Aaron was quite close to his mother. I recall seeing her only once, but I am not sure if it was in person or in a picture in the obituary pages. She was a fine, attractive woman in clothes from the mid-sixties and a poof hairdo. Her name was Rachel, and because I knew Aaron, I always felt I knew her too.

Aaron's sensitivity to the loss of his mother turned from sadness, to anger, to downright meanness. He became a bully of sorts. When my mother was working and unable to pick me up after school, I would leave William W. Smith Elementary School and head to my baby sitter's house on Mansion Way, around the corner from Aaron's house on Winnipeg Street. The way I walked there was the same way he went home. Their homes were on a side of town opposite from mine. Going there was like walking through foreign territory. I felt out of place and like I did not belong in their neighborhood. In order to get to my babysitter's, I would walk one block from school, cross Main Street and pass a corner Shell gas station. Then I would walk one long, seemingly endless block past dilapidated homes, a car repair shop wreaking of oil and burnt tire rubber, and a liquor store smelling of fermented whisky and pee. Upon reaching the far corner convenience store, I would take one sharp left turn and walk two houses over to the house of Cousin Gene, my babysitter. I felt relatively safe once there. That feeling of safety was hard-fought to win some days, however. Aaron knew my routine, and on days of trekking across town, he was right there behind me. One particular trek remains vivid in my memory. I do not recall the trashy homes, junk cars or urine and vomit stench outside the liquor store nearly as much as I remember running for my life that afternoon.

I had said something really mean to Aaron at recess, and he had threatened to beat me up after school. Later, the dismissal bell ominously rang, and it was time to go. My mother could not pick me up that day, so I walked with Josephine, one of my classmates, who lived near Cousin Gene and directly across the street from Aaron. After collecting our book bags and jackets from the cloak room, Josephine and I met outside and headed on. Aaron had left school immediately after the bell and was nowhere to be seen. Merrily walking the short block from school to Main Street with Josephine, I felt light and easy, with no fear of running into Aaron, thinking he was long gone. We passed Donald and Donna's house. They were twins in our grade who lived only a half block from school. They were already home, sitting on the porch. Josephine and I waved to them in passing and continued to the end of the block.

Josephine was a big girl, and smart too. She had three brothers she wrestled with often, so she was also very strong. I felt especially safe walking with her through her neighborhood because everyone knew her. As she greeted people and called out their names, I'd say hi too. This helped me feel more relaxed and comfortable. We crossed Main Street at the light and headed towards the Shell station. No sooner did we pass the gas pumps than out jumped Aaron from behind the car window washer-stand. He'd been waiting for us. I was startled, but Josephine wasn't. Her brothers and the Waters boys were very good friends. Aaron was like a brother to her. Since she was calm, I acted calm too.

Josephine spoke. "Ah, Aaron, what's happening?"

He responded, "Not much. I just made a quick trip to Grand Union." Grand Union was a large grocery store about a block and a half from school. "Can I join you?" Aaron continued.

"Sure, come on," Josephine invited him, having no idea of his threat to get me after school.

Aaron chuckled, looking at me with an 'I'm going to get you now' glare. I was nervous but did not show it. He would not dare bother me with Josephine there. He was big, but she was strong and could pound him well if he acted up. He knew it, too, and held off on bothering me. I paid no attention to the neighborhood infrastructure during the entire walk for keeping my peripherals on Aaron. We reached the street-end in little time. "I'm going to get some Bazooka Bubble Gum." Josephine said as she went into the corner convenience store.

The minute she was out of sight, I stuck my tongue out at Aaron and dashed. He growled and jumped at me. He began chasing me, wielding a toy pocket knife he had just gotten from the bubble gum machine at Grand Union. "I'm gonna kill you!" He threatened, chasing me.

Cousin Gene was waiting at the window for me. I ran up the steps to her front door, turned around and blew my tongue out at Aaron. "Na, na,

same day Aaron chose to walk the fifteen-minute journey from his house to mine. He either still intended to make good on his warning from elementary school, or he just needed to make it known somehow that he really liked me. Whatever his reason for coming over, he wanted to do something mischievous, but had no plan in mind.

Upon arriving at my house, Aaron saw the Era sample hanging in a plastic bag on the door and instantly thought of the thing to do. He opened the container and poured the liquid out on the porch for my family to slip on or, better, for us to have to clean up. When my father returned home from work, he went to retrieve the mail as usual at the front door mailbox and found our neatly kept porch covered with thickened, deep-blue liquid soap. Aaron was long gone by the time we discovered the mess. We found out that he was the culprit because, when we called his house later that day to ask, he confessed to his father. His revenge backfired. Within an hour after the conversation between our fathers, Aaron was on his hands and knees scrubbing and rinsing suds off our porch and out of the front yard. All the wiping and washing away of his sins did not at all make up for my mother missing her free sample of Era, however. She enjoyed getting free stuff as much as I imagined she would be thrilled to win the lottery and was thoroughly disappointed and vocally upset about not having the Era detergent. You'd think someone had died! All kidding aside, Mommy was the most perfect mother. She'd do anything for her family and deserved the best, which included a free sample of Era liquid laundry detergent.

After the Era soap incident, the super-clean porch was graced by Aaron's presence again many times. Aaron and I had become friendlier by our early middle school days, and we'd talk often on the phone after school when homework was completed. Our calls had to end at eight o'clock, which always seemed too short and unfinished. To continue talking, Aaron would tread the familiar path from Winnipeg to Glenn. His arrival was timed for long after my parents had turned in. He'd toss a couple of pebbles to tap my bedroom window pane, signaling that he had arrived. Upon seeing me in pajamas at the window, Aaron would climb to the top of the front porch overhang. I would then open the window for us to continue our conversation, with me sitting on my bed pushed up against the windowed wall and him perched on the porch roof.

When the moon was full and glowing on our talk nights, Aaron appeared sitting bold and confident, illuminated before a lustrous blue backdrop of twinkling stars in the dark sky. We chatted in the midst of what I would later—as an art historian and wholehearted romantic—describe as a "Van Gogh-Starry Night" backdrop. We would talk about a whole lot of nothing and a little bit of everything on those moonlit talk nights. The conversation topics were fun but not as important as the company. What mattered was that we were together. We were in our own private world inhabited only by each other. The fact that my parents were downstairs in their bedroom and my sister was across the upstairs hall in hers was of concern only when we had to control ourselves from laughing too loud. Those evenings were magical, harmless, adventuresome, and filled with never-ending childhood mischief and romance.

Middle School Dance

He asked me to the eighth grade middle school dance, and I said yes. In addition to the late-evening conversation rendezvous at my house, Aaron and I saw each other when walking in the halls at school, while sitting and chatting with friends on the bleachers by the pool, and sometimes at Friendly's ice cream parlor, but this dance would be different. We were officially going on our first date—though we were not yet "officially" a couple.

I wore my favorite adolescent formal dress. It was a second-hand store treasure found by my mother. The bright pink dress had big white polka-dots. It was form fitting at the bodice with a belled full-length skirt. It came with a huge matching hair bow that I wore in the half-up portion of a half-up, half-down hairdo. I looked like my favorite cartoon character, Minnie Mouse, whenever I wore it, and felt simply adorable.

It was about half past six when Aaron was dropped off at my house by his father. He was finely dressed in a medium silver-gray suit, black shoes and black dress socks with a grey, white, and blue thin-striped tie on a crisp white shirt. He looked sharp. I could not let him know that is what I thought, though, as I was still in the persnickety "eeeww, you're a boy" stage. My mother later told me what had occurred when I was getting ready. It went something like this:

"Oooh, Aaron, you are so handsome!" Mommy complimented.
Aaron smiled shyly and replied, "Thank you, Mrs. Crawford."
Mommy said, "Have a seat. Carol will be right down."

My mother directed Aaron to a chair in the kitchen. He walked to it and sat down. I was upstairs being zipped up by my sister while looking in the mirror, touching up my low curls and making sure the bow was straight on the up section of my hair. "You look beautiful, Carol. Are you ready to go down? I think I heard Aaron." My sister, Chy—Chy is her nickname, short for Charlene—smoothed down the back of my dress to flatten it and looked at me as I looked at myself in the mirror. I smiled, exhaled and said, "Yes, I am ready. Let's go."

I walked down and turned the corner from the end of the stairs and saw my father snapping a picture of Aaron leaned over his legs with elbows resting on top. His hands were clasped. Aaron looked in my direction with eager eyes and sat up to see me fully as I walked through the dining room towards him. He was fully standing by the time I reached the kitchen. "You look beautiful. I love the dress," he said with a huge smile.

I bashfully responded, "Thank you," but held off on expressing my full excitement because Mommy, Daddy and Chy were right there.

"The dance begins in five minutes. You two ready to go?" My father looked at the kitchen clock, then at Aaron and me, and started heading for the back door. "I'll be right back, Betty," my father addressed my mother.

Daddy headed out the door. Aaron and I followed him, and we all got in the car for the two-minute ride to Poughkeepsie Middle School.

I never saw the gymnasium look as magically beautiful as it did that night. The pull-up strength endurance ropes were out of sight. The bleachers were pushed back against the wall, and the basketball hoops were folded to the ceiling. Mr. Black, the head custodian, had rigged the room with strobe lights and a mirror ball to reflect and sparkle from the rainbow-blue, fuchsia, and yellow lights illuminating the scene. It looked marvelous, and the jumping music set the atmosphere off right. Mr. Black moonlighted as a DJ, and knew all the tunes us kids liked to dance to. From Kool and the Gang's "Jungle Boogie" to "Strawberry Letter 23" by the Brothers Johnson, to Ohio Players' "Rollercoaster", to "Minute by Minute" by the Doobie Brothers, Mr. Black had all the popular songs from the mid-1970s playing that night. The evening was fun and jumping, like a happy-adolescent dream. I laughed and danced with my girlfriends between dances with Aaron and enjoyed cool ginger ale-punch refreshment drinks. I loved that we had all gotten dressed up that night and come together to get down. At about a quarter to nine, Mr. Black started playing the lighter slow jams to end the night. The dance floor emptied somewhat, and it was easy to spot me with some friends at the punch bowl table, munching on potato chips.

The night could not end without a close "slow grind" dance. Aaron was my date, and he was very proud to be seen with me. He had every right to ask me for a final dance to show off his conquest as well as his affection. Aaron walked to me, took my hand and led me to the dance floor. This was the first time I felt like Cinderella in his presence, with him as my knight in shining armor. "Zoom" by the Commodores was playing. That was my favorite song, and Aaron knew it. He wrapped his arms around my waist. I put mine around his neck. We were close but with an eenie-teenie-weenie bit of breathing space between us. Aaron pulled me closer. I enjoyed the feeling and his bologna scent—to be explained later—so much. "Zoom" ended, and "Always and Forever" by Heatwave began playing immediately afterwards. We kept dancing and holding each other, and did not let go until the song was over and the full lights came on.

Visiting Winnipeg

Because my father did not approve of us being together—except on a special occasion, like the Middle School Dance—I would sneak around to be with Aaron. I would ride my bike to the other side of town to see him. On one occasion I went into his house, though I knew my father would not approve. His widower father, Bernard Waters, was home that day. He was in the kitchen, sitting at the table reading a newspaper while dinner was in the oven. So, it wasn't like we could do anything prohibitive—not yet anyway.

Aaron and I convened in Aaron's bedroom. I sat on his desk chair, picked up a Marvel Comics magazine lying on top of the desk, and pretended to be interested in it. He sat on the edge of his bed, banging his heels against the foot rail while tossing a baseball from a mitt. "I got to go out to the store to get some bread," Mr. Waters called. The chair slid over the kitchen linoleum as he got up. Then, the back door slammed shut. I continued to look at a Spiderman strip. We heard the engine start and the car move slowly over the gravel driveway towards the street. Aaron did not waste time. He grabbed my wrist and gently pulled me to him. I willingly went. Before long, we were at the head of his bed, holding each other and kissing, with him unbuttoning my shirt. My father knew me well and was right to be concerned about how close I'd get to Aaron—or, at the very least, he accurately anticipated the acts of young affection. After all, he was a kid once, and Mr. Waters was a kid once, too!

Bam, Bam. We heard the pounding, stopped immediately, sat up, and looked at the door. Mr. Waters had quietly returned, loudly knocked at Aaron's bedroom door, then began to open it. I never saw a pudgy little fella move so fast! Aaron jumped up and blocked the door as his father tried to enter. Frantically covering my exposed torso, I scrambled for my shirt, jumped up off the bed, put the shirt on and buttoned up out of view.

"Boy, are you crazy? What's wrong with you? Don't you push me out!" Mr. Waters demanded, trying to open the door. Aaron saw that I was covered and released the door. Wide-eyed and guilty with a racing heart, I could barely look at Mr. Waters. Aaron was obviously scared. "It's time for you to go home, young lady," Mr. Waters said, peering at me and pointing out the door. He did not need to say another word. I cowered my way between him and the door frame, dashed across the kitchen and out the back door, got on my bike and zipped on home.

As adults, Aaron and I talked and laughed about that time. He said he and his father also had a good laugh years later. Something had told Mr. Waters he could not trust us to be left alone, so he quietly returned to find us engaged as anticipated. Mr. Waters also knew how much his son was infatuated with me and advised Aaron he did not stand a chance with me because of my father.

Duchess County Fair

My parents agreed to let us go to the fair together only if my sister drove. That was fine with me as it would allow us time with each other. I sat in the front passenger seat. Aaron sat in the back. We made faces at each other through the side rear view mirror. Chy, Aaron and I talked intermittently about trivial things during the half-hour drive. We named the rides we'd go on and who we might see there. It was a comfortably warm August night. I wore blue denim carpenter pants and a pink tank top with my favorite flat-footed popsicle-grape purple Pro Keds. I had bought the colorful sneakers at Haberdashery's on the downtown Poughkeepsie Main Street walking mall. Aaron had on a white t-shirt and blue jeans. I do not recall the make of his shoes per se, but they were black and white and most likely Converse All Stars. All the cool boys wore Converses in the late 1970s. On the drive, Aaron told me Franklin and Annette would be there. They were boyfriend and girlfriend and two grades above us. Franklin was Aaron's good friend. Annette's cousin, Davis, was a boy I had gone with briefly before finally agreeing to go steady with Aaron. Davis was also Aaron's best friend.

I had agreed to go with Davis because I was flattered to be asked by him, and I thought he was kind of cute. He actually liked a girl named Cora, and I figured Aaron had dared Davis to ask me to go with him so he could keep a closer eye on me—that is why I couldn't understand why Aaron was so upset and jealous when he heard Davis and I were going together. Davis and I had absolutely nothing in common. Our relationship and times together amounted to conversation on the phone while he smacked on oranges and read wrestling magazines. When we were not on the phone, we were in each other's vicinity during school, at afterschool track practices and meets, or at the pool. On those rare occasions when we saw each other, we avoided one another like the plague, or Aaron was right there to watch us, making sure Davis and I did not do anything that Aaron wanted to do with me. Kissing Davis was out. Walking with him hand-in-hand up the school hall was of no interest to me and too embarrassing to consider. Kids in my town were not that publicly bold back in the late 1970s—except on the middle school dance floor. Meeting Davis at McDonald's or somewhere to eat just never happened. Davis and I were boyfriend and girlfriend in name only. I forgot how it ended, but it did. When Aaron found out Davis and I had broken up, he officially asked me to be his girlfriend, and I said yes. Now that Aaron and I were going together, we openly did couple things. Going to the Duchess County Fair was our second official date or, actually, more like our first official date, since Aaron and I were finally officially going together.

The scents of roasted peanuts, caramel popcorn, cotton candy, candied apples and manure filled the air. It was turning dusk, and flashing lights were seen in the distance. We parked and got out of my mother's burnt-orange 1970 Ford Camaro in a cow pasture-turned-parking lot and headed towards the commotion. Once in closer proximity to the festivities, I heard the ding of bells following the sound of a hammer hitting the trigger at the Strong Man game. We had made it to the fair. Chy ran into her friends

Gloria, Geoff and Anna and went off with them after Aaron and I agreed to meet her at the exit gate at ten o'clock. We went off to wander the fairgrounds and came upon the ring toss game booth. I hoped Aaron would be drawn to try and win me a gigantic stuffed orange bear that had caught my eye. "Oooo, look at that bear! It is my favorite color, too!" I pointed, nudging him towards the booth.

"So, I guess you want me to try and win that for you," he said with a grin. "Do I get a kiss if I get it?" I instantly understood what he was grinning about. It had taken me forever to say yes and publicly admit I was going with Aaron, and now he wanted a kiss from me in front of everyone!

"Win it first. We'll see." I responded with no promise.

"Three rings for a dollar! Three rings for a dollar! Land the ring on the bottle and win!" The attendant repeated his call, which got louder as we approached the booth. He knew there was another sucker about to bite. The wooden rings all over the hay-covered ground and a token ring around a bottle neck here and there implied that the game was not an easy win, but it could be done. To prove it, the attendant tossed a ring just as we arrived for us to see it land on a bottle neck. If the bespectacled wimp of an attendant could do it, the robust Aaron figured he was a sure shot, and he bit. Five dollars and fifteen rings later, I had no bear to take home and Aaron did not get a kiss. We moved on through the fair.

"Yeooooow! Weeeeeeee!" Screeches, hollers, and screams were heard from the roller coaster ride as Aaron pulled me towards it. I did not resist, for I was eager to go. I loved roller coasters and relished the chance to sound my blood-curdling scream when zooming down a sudden drop after mounting to careen over a breathtaking pinnacle. It was also a chance for Aaron to hold me protectively, while we sat side-by-side. I loved his tight, close holds. They were always warm, comforting, and delicious moments to look forward to. He smelled like cold cuts, which I will explain here as I earlier promised: "Eau de cold cuts or bologna" was the common adolescent boy scent that lingered at the locker of every male student in middle school who could have used more deodorant.

We each forked over fifty cents and stood in the short line. Next go round would be our turn. Our bodies were close, but we were careful not to touch when standing in line. For heaven sakes, touching was absolutely out of the question. It was one step removed from one of his private hairs falling off and somehow wiggling its way down his pants and up my panties—I once thought the sperm in the eighth grade health book pictures were pubic hairs. Next thing I knew, I'd be pregnant! How in the world would I explain THAT to my father when he did not like the idea of me being with Aaron in the first place?! I used to think Daddy did not approve of us being together because Aaron was from the north side of town, because he was too rough and tough, and because he was not gentleman enough for daddy's little girl. As I matured, I came to believe that my father did not like him for the simple fact that Aaron was a boy and he liked me, period. The frowns, the looks and the glares my father gave Aaron every time he came around were intimidating to say the least. Any boy would be scared. Heck! I was taken aback by my father's snarls and grunts. I later thought he acted that way because he did not want me to get too involved, or sexually active, and wind up pregnant. My father never said as much, but his two younger sisters and an older one, too, got pregnant out of wedlock. The younger ones married the fathers, but my older aunt did not marry either father of her two beautiful children. Such happenstance is commonplace today, but I imagine it was frowned upon and given a scarlet letter of the capital kind in his small southern hometown fifty-plus years ago. In my teen years, I fathomed Daddy could not live with the stigma of one of his daughters having an illegitimate child.

By the time the empty roller coaster car rounded to us my silly concerns about having a baby should Aaron and I touch, had faded. We hopped on board the car and were met by an attendant who lowered a thick metal single bar over our heads and began to secure belts across our waists. Aaron slid close to me before we were fastened in. We would inevitably touch, and my wild child imagination had me destined to spend the rest of my life with Aaron, pregnant and raising babies. We had a roller coaster ride to enjoy first, so I abandoned my worries and cleared my throat to be ready for a high-pitched scream.

With all riders safely fastened in their seats, the train of cars scuttled forward. What began as an image of bravery, with me sitting erect, holding tightly onto the bar on top of the seat in front of us, ended in picture-perfect chivalry with Aaron holding me firmly and my head buried in his chest, peeking between my balled fists. Somewhere between the start and the finish, I threw my hands up in the air, let off my vibrant scream, then lost all boldness and dove into the bosom of my bear to feel safe and protected. It was no joke, and I was not pretending. I really got scared! Bold, bad Carol needed the protective embrace of her cuddling bear's bologna-scented hold. It was deliciously comforting and exactly what I needed for the scary ride to transform into a mere bumpy journey in a metallic box through my imagined romance-land that ended all too soon.

Aaron spotted Franklin and Annette when we exited after the ride ended. They were walking arm in arm, sharing a cone of cotton candy. "Yo, Frank," Aaron maturely roared. Franklin looked over his shoulder, acknowledged Aaron, and the couple turned and walked our way.

"What's up, A? Hey, Carol!" Franklin called to us while walking over. The guys shook hands. Annette and I said hello and hugged. "We're going to the Ferris wheel. Want to join us?" Franklin asked.

"This is so cool!!!!" I thought. Excitement instantly popped up in my mind bubble. Franklin and Annette were okay with meeting Aaron and me and us joining in on their fun. They did not say, "Eeewww," or give me a disgusted look for being with Aaron the way other kids at school did—I know now the other kids reacted that way because they were jealous. The notion of Aaron and me was accepted so easily by Franklin and Annette. That was wonderful! It was time to let my paranoid guard down, step out of the peer pressure cooker overheating in my thirteen-years-young mind, and go have some worriless fun. I liked Aaron a lot, and it was past due time to publicly enjoy his company.

I appreciated the attention Aaron gave me and the pedestal he put me on, but I always wanted him to see himself as my equal, and I told him this many times. That way we could compatibly be together. He harbored the delusion that my sister and I were saints who needed to remain pure and untouched. I know that was the message of the insistent vibes my father generated. Aaron felt the energy clearly. He never took advantage of me nor forced me to do anything I was uncomfortable with doing. I loved him for that, too. If either of us was a saint, though, it was Chy for sure, not me. I loved kissing tenderly and sharing love passionately—the later came in my adult years, of course. Tender kisses are what Aaron and I shared as often as possible, and as privately as possible—considering the kiss we shared as adults in my friends' apartment in New York, little changed in that respect.

We spent that entire August evening at the fair having pure fun, laughing, eating tasty junk foods and sweets, and grabbing each other for dear life on scary rides. We spent a ton of money on games only to win and leave with a Duchess County Fair pennant and a fuchsia-haired miniature gnome. When it was almost ten o'clock, we headed to the exit to meet up with my sister and leave. During the ride home, Aaron and I sat in the back seat together. The kiss he had been hoping to earn earlier by winning an orange bear would soon be his. Because kissing privately was our thing, for some reason we thought it possible to kiss privately with Chy driving. Upon reaching Route 9G, Aaron and I were at it with great gusto, with "Saint Chy" glancing, on occasion, in the rear view mirror. Shocked and numb, all she could say after we had dropped Aaron off at his home was, "I saw what you and Aaron were doing."

I am not sure how I thought it could be missed, but I was surprised that she had seen and simply replied, "Please don't tell." Even more strange was that as passionate as we were that night and so many other times together, Aaron and I never ever shared love. But we came very close to it when I embarked on a professional dance career.

Dance Theatre of Harlem and Living in New York City

After attending a six-week Dance Theatre of Harlem (DTH) summer intensive in the fall of 1978, I left Poughkeepsie to dance with the DTH Company as an apprentice. Co-directors Arthur Mitchell and Karel Shook, along with the DTH school administrator, Shirley Mills, made arrangements for me to complete my preparatory education at Professional Children's School and invited me to live in New York City. I was age fourteen-going-on-fifteen and in my tenth-grade year of high school. After the intensive and receiving invitation to move to New York City, I cried with joy during the ninety-minute-drive back home to Poughkeepsie. Thinking about the victorious dream-come-true offer overwhelmed me to tears. Daddy was driving, and Mommy was in the front passenger seat. In the quiet between my sniffles, I heard sobbing. I looked at my father in the rear-view mirror and saw tears streaming down his face. Suddenly, I realized that the news of the invitation had hit him as if it were his victory, too. My father played a huge role in me embarking on a professional dance career. He sought advice on what to do with my undeniable passion for dance. One of his co-workers suggested we seek professional opportunities in New York City. This led me to DTH. It is due to Daddy's inquiry and my mother and father's support and follow-up back then that I am a dancer and dance teacher today—I am forever grateful to Mommy and Daddy, as they helped me realize my dream.

I left my friends and family behind when I moved to New York City, but my heart was still Aaron's, and his was mine. Aaron visited me often at the DTH headquarters at 466 W 152ND Street and at my New York apartment by traveling on the Metro North train down the Hudson River on past the Harlem River. The train made local stops from Poughkeepsie. Tremont Avenue on the Harlem River was my stop on route. On many a night, I would look out my window over the Harlem River and watch Aaron exit the train, climb the steps and walk up the hill to my building.

Soon after, the buzz of the intercom would sound. Without asking who it was, I would press the button to unlock the security door in the lobby. My apartment, #4A, was on the fourth floor to the immediate left of the elevator. I would listen at my door to hear the elevator door open, and peep through the apartment door hole. Upon Aaron's stepping off, I would unchain, unlock and open the door, and let him in.

Having Aaron in my apartment was no big deal to me. It was actually a relief. I felt especially safe and secure with Aaron around because he loved and protected me. At age fifteen, living alone in the big city can be very scary once mind-chatter about all the harmful things that can happen begins. Someone could break into my apartment when I was out, hide and wait for me to return. Upon getting home, who knows what could happen? When Aaron was on his way and finally with me such negative and uncertain thoughts dissolved. Together we would pop popcorn and melt butter in the same cast-iron skillet I had made grilled cheese sandwiches in earlier for dinner. One night, a major network was airing the annual broadcast of *The Wizard of Oz.* With corn popped, buttered and salted, we sat on my love seat with the snack in a bowl on our laps and cuddled to watch the movie. It always felt right being alone and in private with Aaron. He'd wrap his arm around my shoulder. I'd lean my head against his, fold up my legs and reach my arm around his belly, then exhale. I was at home in dwelling, mind, body and spirit. Nothing should interrupt such an occasion, especially not a call or visit from my father. So before I could get too settled, I made my nightly call home. The number, (914) 452-5602, was the combination to dial for a comforting pep talk when I did not feel good about myself for not being the thinnest girl in the DTH Company. Those were also the digits to dial when money was running low and I needed to grocery shop or wanted to see a movie. Most importantly that night, it was the ticket to a magical time with Aaron. One call picked up by my folks two hours away meant Aaron and I were home free! Fortunately, my folks were home, and I could relax. Soon after the call home, the bowl of popcorn was a quarter empty, Miss Almira Gulch had turned from a woman riding her bike through the tornado into the Wicked Witch of the West, flying on a broom with wind pulling her hair and flapping her cloak, and Aaron and I were hotly and heavily making out and feeling on each other freely. Seemingly endless passionate kissing was what we did, and before too long the teenage sensations in our bodies were fully responding—tell-tale signs that we were ready for more. But because we were both virgins, we did not fully understand what "more" looked like.

It was getting late and near time for Aaron to leave to catch the one o'clock train home. Oh, but the kissing, the touching and the feeling were so wonderful. It felt so good that we could not stop, and he missed the last train. Missing his ride home meant getting up extra early to get to school on time. We eventually came up for air, dealt with reality and stopped. He pulled the single bed out from the love seat. I went and got some sheets from the bathroom closet for him to make his bed. School started at eight o'clock for me, and I needed to leave by ten minutes to seven to make it on time via NYC mass transit. The best Metro North train for Aaron to catch to get to his school, which also began at eight o'clock, was at six o'clock. We had to get some sleep.

I could get ready for bed in no time at all. So I left him fitting the sheets on the pull-out bed in the living room and headed for the bathroom to brush my teeth and wash my face. From the bathroom, I took one short step to my right to my bedroom and closed the door to get dressed for bed while Aaron fumbled around in the living room down the short hall. I began putting on my pajamas, and shortly thereafter I heard a knock at the door.

"Yes?" I asked, knowing perfectly well it was Aaron.

"Can I come in?" He asked.

"Wait a minute, please," I responded while quickly buttoning my pajama top. "Come in. I'm done." Aaron entered with a gleam in his eye and a dreamy look on his face. With arms slowly reaching, he walked to me, took me and held me tight. I wrapped my arms around his neck, and we began to kiss earnestly. Slowly, we "danced", taking steps in unison towards my bed until the back of my legs touched the side of the mattress. He carefully lowered me to the bed, and we maneuvered to lie vertically with my head resting on the pillow and he on top of me. We enjoyed each other with the greatest passion but, again, did not know exactly what to do with that passion other than to keep kissing and take our clothes off. So that is exactly what we did with tremendous delight.

When we were both fully disrobed, Aaron stopped kissing me and began to examine my body. He studied and traced the circumference of my bosom with his fingers, a little like when the head sewer at DTH would draw the outer circle of my breast with chalk on fabric pressed against my chest in preparation to build a bodice for a costume. I always held my stomach in on such occasions, and it was so uncomfortable. The time with Aaron was very different and unique in that Aaron also gracefully drew his fingers in a sinuous line down my front and side across my rib cage to my waist but with no objective of making an outfit for me to wear. He did it to help me feel very warm and wonderful inside. I had been topless in front of Aaron in the past, but this was different. We were not in his bedroom rushing to make out before his father returned from the store. This time was not like when he leaned me against the wall of the nearby elementary school on the way home from a weekend evening birthday party. We pulled my top up that time so he could kiss my body, and I had barely made my ten o'clock curfew that night. Nor was it like the time he sneaked into the girls' locker room at the Y when the coast was clear and joined me in the shower to help rinse off pool chlorine between our kisses. To the contrary, the time alone in my apartment that night was completely free of worry of getting caught. We could do whatever we wanted, and the only thing that could stop us were our consciences, if we allowed them.

We lay feeling and touching one another, unrushed for the first time. When satisfied with these deliberate acts, Aaron re-positioned himself on top, kissing me. Then he consciously stopped, pulled back to look at me, and resumed holding and kissing me. That is as far as we went that night or ever. Aaron and I would never again be that close to experiencing an all-inclusive physical love. I was apprehensive about going all the way, and he did not want to force me, so he halted our affections that evening. It was two o'clock in the morning and way past bedtime for both of us. Aaron respectfully quit and headed for his bed in the living room. I fully draped the covers over me, snuggled up, and fell asleep.

Daylight danced over the Harlem River through my bedroom window and covered my resting, blanketed-body. When fully awake, I sat up in bed to get a better look outside. To my pleasant surprise, Aaron was laying down asleep on the floor, wrapped in a blanket with his head on a pillow in the three feet of floor space between my bed and the windowed wall. I felt so much love for him at that moment. He had returned to my room while I lay soundly and peacefully sleeping. I imagine he entered to make sure I was alright. While studying me, he must have contemplated what it was like to lie next to me and for us to fall asleep in one another's arms. We'd feel each other breathing and know we were safe and protected by the divine love that united us—the divine love that no doubt created us for each other.

That slumbering experience that I imagined Aaron and me to have had was one never realized in our lifetime. I eventually broke it off with Aaron—fool that I was, as I believe he was the best person for me for life. I just did not see it at the time. For him, I was the one. He would have done anything for me, become anything I asked him to be. I was his everything, but he knew I could not settle down. I was too young and was actively pursuing a professional dance career. There was a world of adventure ahead of me that he could not provide nor deprive me of experiencing. The breakup

Dublin, Ireland; July 1979

occurred three years into my new life and world of dancing with Dance Theatre of Harlem. As devastated as Aaron was, he accepted my decision and we parted.

Turin, Italy, July 1982

My new existence was far removed and different from the ginger ale, fruit punch and potato chip middle school dances adorned with crinkled-paper streamers, confetti and inflated balloons. My new life as a budding professional dancer was so unlike the once upon a time, risky, quiet, front porch awning conversations under starry nights and crescent moons. My state of being became wine-champagne-hors-d'oeuvre receptions after worldwide performances and strolling on dirt roads alongside wheat fields outside my hotel in Spoleto and walking over the Po River in Turin, when on tour in Italy.

Kennedy Center for the Performing Arts, Washington, D. C., February 1987

The emotional and spiritual maturity I gained in days and weeks, months and years that included sailing the English Channel between London and Ireland and climbing hundreds of steps to stretch my arms—for a photo—like the Christo Redentor statue in Rio de Jeneiro, Brazil, while performing internationally, was best achieved without Aaron waiting for me back home. With each flight overseas and bus tour across the country, I was becoming different. I was changing and growing each time the curtain closed on the *Firebird* ballet crescendo, or when the curtain closed on the *Dougla* ballet procession, followed by the stride of a man stopping mid-stage, then trice-pounding and balancing chest and chin accented high, with straight arm thrust side parallel to the floor. I grew and changed as sure as sets change between *Creole Giselle* acts and Little Lizzie Borden becomes an adult in the life-course of the *Fall River Legend* ballet. I matured and developed fundamentally, as well as artistically, on the road and on the stage. Life altered for me in the world of privileged-theater and make-believe-ballet. On any given day on any given stage, I could be a fiercely-attacking, blue-unitard clad ballerina in John McFall's *Toccata e Due Canzoni*, or Stella in *A Streetcar Named Desire*, or a Grande Battemente girl in Balanchine's *Four Temperaments*, or a chiffon-skirt clad girl hopping in pointe shoes in *Concerto Barocco*. The momentum was high on the costume-changing, pointe-shoe-breaking Dance Theatre of Harlem roller coaster ride, especially when performing the romantically playful pas de trois in the second movement of Billy Wilson's *Concerto in F.*

Concerto in F, October 1987

Moscow, Russia, May 1988

In the wonderment of travelling and performing, I was shouting internally with fierce glee, and I became forever more wise and brave. I simply was not the same. I was well embarked on my life's journey of worldwide splendor and magnificence, dancing before hundreds of thousands of people from royalty to commoner.

Correspondingly, I would become even more removed from Aaron and my "country bumpkin" Poughkeepsie persona upon moving out of the Tremont Avenue love nest and on to Fordham Hills—another New York City piece of the pie, a la "The Jeffersons."

Hello, Fordham Hills

My lovely one-bedroom Tremont Avenue apartment in New York City was more than adequate for a small-town teen turning young woman from Poughkeepsie. I enjoyed playing adult and house there—especially when Aaron visited. It was maturing fun to arrange plates, bowls, cups and glasses in the kitchen cabinets and organize a set of silverware, including a lone steak knife, in the utensil drawer. I felt grown, and no one could tell me differently—except for my father, who warned me in no uncertain terms that I was never to have male company there, and if I did have a boy there, that was it! I'd be packed up and shipped home. No questions asked. Good-bye, New York! Well, now Daddy knows that I did have a boy in my Tremont Avenue apartment, and moved on to Fordham Hills to have a boy there, too!

By age seventeen, I felt more stable and sure of what I wanted and where I was going. My apprenticeship with the company turned from a $75.00 a week stipend to a whopping $250.00 a week salary as a full company member, with no benefits, but per diem on the road, which I saved and invested in real estate. By age eighteen, I was in a love affair with a man named Bobby from California. He was in the Dance Theatre of Harlem Company as well. One night of romance when on tour turned to three years of dating to three years of marriage to three years of separation and, ultimately, divorce. I married Bobby because I wanted to live with him without opposition from my father. When I told my father I wanted to live with the man, his response was something along the lines of, "Are you crazy?!!" or "What would your little cousins think?" Here I was trying to do the right thing by seeking permission, as my "honor and respect" ethics told me was the right thing to do. I'd ask for permission to live with Bobby in hopes of receiving approval with a blessing. Instead, I got the guilt-loaded "you are insane" response with a reprimand to consider my younger relatives, who looked up to me. After shaking off my wings the flood of disapproval meant to discourage and silence me, I gave Bobby the okay to pack his things and move in.

The first couple of years living in the studio cooperative apartment at Fordham Hills were intense. Bobby and I shacked up and tried to make the place our home with two Siamese cats and a gold fish in a glass bowl. As comfortable as we tried to be in "our place," there was always a ghostly fear of my father showing up. And, appearing unannounced one night is exactly what Daddy did.

Daddy left Mondale Ave unsettled as to what to do— Mondale Ave is the name of the street we had moved to in Poughkeepsie at the time I began dancing with DTH. Daddy and Mommy had an argument, and he got in the car and headed down the Taconic Parkway. Two hours later Daddy was knocking at my door. I answered the door and let my father in. Bobby had gone to the bathroom.

"Your mother kicked me out of the house," Daddy reported while walking in. Confused and sympathetic, I followed him the short distance from the front door to the living room. Daddy sat down on the couch, looking pitiful and at a loss. When Bobby came out of the bathroom, my father perked up. "What are you doing here?!!" Daddy furiously asked.

"I live here," Bobby responded.

Angry and frantic, my father grabbed an empty bottle nearby, slammed it on the living room floor and threatened Bobby with the jagged edges. "Oh, no you don't!" Daddy shouted, wielding the broken bottle at Bobby and threatening him. Scared and shaken, Bobby ran to the door and left. I was shocked and told my father to leave. I went into the kitchen when he left, closed the door, called my mother and then sat on the floor. Mommy and I talked until dawn when the rising sun lit the layered beds of clouds pink and blue. She told me about the argument.

"He became so frantic," Mommy told me decades later of the confrontation leading my father to leave Poughkeepsie and head to my apartment. That occurred back in 1984, and, according to my mother, she did not kick him out of the house. Items were thrown during the argument, including her favorite vase, which was broken. My mother evolved strong and firm on her intolerance of what they argued about, and the two are still together after fifty-six years. He is now seventy-eight and she is eighty—always honoring their vow "until death do us part." All I can say is "God bless them" and hope to learn from their example.

Getting Married

I take responsibility for my father expecting me to conform to his desires for me because I did not assert myself and lived to please him for so long. That had to change, however. So when he did not approve of me living with Bobby, and when he broke a bottle, threatening to hurt the man, getting married was my recourse for asserting my independence, living with Bobby and being left alone. I reasoned that if Bobby were the man of the house and the man in my life, my father would have no choice but to leave us alone. I knew that another male being the man in my life was exactly what my father had feared. I reasoned that my father would have to face that fear and deal with it when, one early August Sunday morning, Bobby and I exchanged marriage vows in a back yard garden wedding at my parent's house in Poughkeepsie. It was 1985. I was 21 years young.

Beyond wanting to live with Bobby in peace, I did wholeheartedly go into the marriage for life, expecting Bobby's and my love to grow strong and remain so. It was a sad and tragic choice on both of our parts to marry, that came from an immature place of fear and assertion. After three years of marriage, Bobby came home one night and told me he did not want to be married anymore. Three months prior to his announcement, I had left Dance Theatre of Harlem. After ten years with the company and at age 24-going-on-25 in 1988, I had reached my personal peak with DTH. I decided to go to college to formally study the art and worldly experiences I had known and seen from mandatory DTH 'culture day' excursions as well as from international banking visits for lire-to-dollar exchanges. Bobby remained with DTH when I left, though. Perhaps my absence from the daily DTH barre and stage performances was too great for him, or, more than likely, he just wanted freedom. Whatever the case, I was devastated by his announcement and felt helpless, not knowing what to do when just three years prior, I had been certain of my actions in getting married and had gotten everyone and everything in place to make it happen.

The Wedding Dress

Prior to the wedding, my bridesmaids, all dance colleagues, and matron of honor, my sister Chy, were due to arrive in Poughkeepsie in three days, and I still needed to pick up my tailored and ready wedding dress. Who could I call to help me get it? Being home in Poughkeepsie always brought on a flood of thoughts, memories, and feelings of earlier days—mid-1960s to early-1980s—with Aaron. I was drawn to call upon my one true love known to date; the man created just for me, who I could always count on and who would do anything for me. So, I called Aaron, and sure enough, to my delight and keen intuition, he was in town! He had returned to the United States about a month earlier with a wife and daughter, age two, in tow. I asked for his help getting the wedding dress, and he happily obliged—I like to think it did not faze him or me that I was about to marry Bobby.

Aaron picked me up at my Mondale Ave Poughkeepsie home. It was such a pleasure to see my old friend. We talked, laughed, and caught each other up on life adventures during the drive to the bridal boutique. I shared facts about my dance life that he already knew. He told me the local paper and news channels overseas had advertised DTH's presence when I was performing and he was stationed in Europe. I was very proud of Aaron for achieving a successful career and life. Prior to becoming a nurse, he had been in the United States Army stationed in Germany. My father was surprised to hear of Aaron being in the army. Daddy never expected Aaron to amount to anything. It makes me mad when my mother, in trying to please my father, gives Daddy the credit for inspiring Aaron to make something of his life. Her comments completely negate the fact, as I perceive it, that her husband did not approve of the love of two young people many decades ago—a love I know she had been in favor of happening, being that she is a hopeful romantic.

Aaron knew of all the places I had toured and told me how he was tempted to surprise me on more than one occasion when I was in Europe in a neighboring country. I thought, and shared with him, that if he had come to see me then, we would have gotten together and our lives would be very different now. We would definitely be married and probably have a child or two. I'd be fat and frumpy looking. I'd resent him for that and start needless fights fueled by the resentment. We would have finally shared love, though, and I would be grateful for that. These simple scenarios were comparable to what Aaron—with his chuckle—thought our lives would have become, as well. For that reason, and because he knew how important it was to me to dance, he stayed away. Besides, he had married young—age 19! So there Aaron and I were, getting a wedding dress for me to wear to marry a man—Bobby—I was convinced I knew and loved, so we could live together. Years later, Aaron and I talked about that trip to the bridal boutique and what it was like seeing me in a dress intended for marrying someone other than him. Wide-eyed and supportive, he thought me the most beautiful sight he had ever seen when I appeared from behind the dressing room curtain in a white gown, swaying and twirling like Cinderella about to go to the ball.

Really Letting Go This Time

As I sit here at age fifty-one, and reflect upon memories of Aaron, I recall many more that could be shared. Each is just as beautiful, making up the pure and true love story between us. I want him with me right now. I want him to come knocking at my back bedroom door in the middle of the night, as he often warned he would do—since we began communicating again as older adults—so he could be with me, and, in my hopes, for us to share the mad passionate love of our dreams and unsaid promises.

I asked him what he thought it would be like for him if and when we finally shared love. What he imagined was going crazy with excitement because he wanted it to happen as much, if not more, than I did. I jokingly told him it would probably happen when we are ninety. We would finally come together then and live a magical and miraculous life together. I told him my desire and dream was for us to one day know endless love with each other—if he were single, of course, and as long as no one was hurt. He agreed.

Sadly, such fantasies would never be the case. Aaron died fifteen months ago from a genetic aneurism, but not before I had already decided three months earlier to let him go—this being a good three and a half years after the "lotion-rub, a-time-to-hold" afternoon in New York that opened this scene. My being pleased to have let Aaron go may sound callous, but letting go was a sincere act of love for him and for his family as much as it was for me. Our conversations were getting dangerous. He said many times, in the course of knowing him, that he would do anything for me because he loved me so much. So, I tested the waters—no pun intended—and asked if he'd leave his wife for me, knowing good and well I could not accept him if he did. His verbal response was, "don't ask me to do that," which he stated again and again after I risked and inquired several more times. I never expected nor wanted him to say yes, and he did not disappoint me. If anything, I came close to disappointing him, which became apparent when he conclusively said, "Carol, you can't ask me to do that. I'd never see my family again." Now that was the Aaron I knew: a responsible, faithful, honest and reliable man. I am quite cognizant of my words and phrasing. The point was intentionally presented as a question, not as a command, to see how it would be perceived and how he would respond. So technically,

I did not act out of character either. With all games put aside, it was not easy to let Aaron go, even when I knew I had to in order to live free and honest. It was necessary to let go in order to make room in my heart for love, existence, and creativity with a special someone yet to be revealed. I know that is what I want and what Aaron wanted for me, but it could not happen until I released my fantasies of Aaron and Carol. So I committed and let go of Aaron on my own at first, and then, ultimately, with no other choice, because he passed.

My life with Aaron helped shape me into who I am today. I am forever grateful to God for giving me this life and allowing me to have experiences that are now long-lasting memories with the boy-turned-man named Aaron, and what our friendship, our relationship, and our love taught me. It taught me that life is meant to have love in it. It taught me a great love between a man and a woman can be spiritual, not physical. Aaron never knew me in a complete physical, sexual way. We never connected through intercourse, yet we knew each other completely through the shared way we had thought and lived. He knew me as well as I know myself. I had expectations of him honoring his word and commitments to his wife and family, and that he did to his dying day. Still, we were here as humans created for each other, and we found love in each other and everyone, regardless of what they did or did not do, and for what they taught us, which in the end is the great lesson of L-O-V-E. I pray everyone is blessed to know love as it is right for them.

Goodbye Aaron. Our love is eternal. Thank you for sharing you and it with me. God blessed me with you. To bless and free us both, I say goodbye and release you, knowing you have ascended to heaven to be with God. I am comforted in knowing you are perfect now and receiving the rest you so greatly deserve.

SCENE 2

Bennett

"Our love was my first adult love, and it took my breath away."

LONG AFTER MY CHILDHOOD LIFE-COURSE journey with Aaron (Circa pre-1971–1981), after and during my short-lived "time-to-grow-up" dating-marriage-separation-divorce experience with Bobby (Circa 1982–1988), and before Aaron and I reconnected to become "best friends" and he died too soon (Circa 2002–2014), there was Bennett (Circa 1989–1991).

Our love was not long ago, and it is not long forgotten. Our love was my first adult love, and it took my breath away. It lasted two years, and it was real and true. Our love was intense, passionate, and beautiful. I saw us spending the rest of our lives together and even suggested it—literally asked him to do just that. I believed a life-long commitment was what I wanted. I believed I could live with him, making the most of us, because our love was incredible, and that was all I needed to know to believe it possible to live magically together forever with him. He did not seem to see it that way, however. Or, maybe he was pretending not to see it or saw something else when I posed the question. His lack of response was ever-present, so I said goodbye. When I left, he thought I'd be back. When I did not return, he realized that what he had taken for granted and given up was gone for good, and it was too late.

Elevated Platform

The south bound #4 arrived at the elevated station stop every day at two minutes past eleven. On this particular Saturday, I would take my metallic chariot to Manhattan, transfer to the A train and make the excursion to SoHo to peruse galleries, walk through stores that sold kitchenware and other household items, and then purchase nuts, a sandwich, and a smoothie at the neighborhood health food store. Oh yeah, and there was the Strand Bookstore to visit. A trek to downtown Manhattan south of Houston Street was not complete until I walked through the shelved aisles of old maps, posters, and dusty books to read an intro, a prologue, or a chapter or two before being forced to leave in a watery-eyed sneezing fit. My allergic intolerance to the mildew, musty odor, and dusty particles floating in the sun-lit air caused me to make an abrupt departure every time I visited the literary Mecca.

Most everyone wore black in SoHo, and many of them appeared to be visual artists. The messy hair, hung-over tired eyes, and turpentine-stained hands with dried paint caked in their fingernails and cuticles made them easy to spot. Having been an assistant to an art teacher-artist who lived in that part of the City and who often taught class with the signature look, I was familiar with the appearance and lifestyle. They were night creatures who ventured into the daylight for fresh air, a quick smoke, and a cup of coffee on their studio stoop after an all-nighter of painting, drinking, and getting stoned. I am an artist who once dreamed of living a life in SoHo—not to live the stereotypical artist lifestyle, but to live in an open-floor high ceiling loft space where I could entertain lots of friends and see everything I owned while moving gracefully from bathroom to bedroom to kitchen to living room, on my way out the accordion-gated entrance door.

This was the scene, the zeitgeist, the 'spirit of the time.' I was on my way on the train to share in the experience, but before I got to the artist dream haven, something happened on the elevated platform. Directly across from me was a man I had seen many times before. He lived on Sherman Avenue in my neighborhood. I had never been up his way because there was never a need for me to go there. I could see the beginning of his street whenever walking through the park that connected onto Fordham Road; still, nothing enticed me to go up there.

I first saw him sitting on a bench near the park entrance that I passed through to get home. He was a honey-brown, tall, medium-built black man with broad shoulders and an angular frame who would relax and sing as he watched and greeted everyone walking by. His voice was sultry and romantic, with a lot of soul. His dark-brown eyes were large, alert, and piercing. We caught each other's eyes, and I stopped to speak.

"Hi, I really enjoy your singing. Are you a musician?" I inquired, seeing a guitar case leaning against the bench next to him.

"Thank you," he responded and continued, "Yeah, I am a musician, singer, and songwriter, too."

I smiled and nodded in approval. "Was that your song you were singing?" I asked.

"Yes," he answered simply. The man clearly had a gift and talent for music.

Whenever I spot a person with talent, I instantly elevate them to star status. "So, where can I get your album?"

He enjoyed my high-spirited, sincere inquiry laughing and saying, "I am working on it now."

I stayed and chatted with him more. He rhetorically asked if I was a dancer. The huge shoulder bag I carried, slew-footed walk, and bun hairstyle gave it away. I told him I danced ballet with Dance Theatre of Harlem—I was still with the company and married to Bobby. He was impressed and said that he wanted to see me dance someday. DTH was about to go on tour to Japan, but we had a New York season coming up in the winter. I promised to remind him of it if we should run into each other again. He said he'd appreciate knowing and would come if he could. We ended our chat and went our separate ways.

I walked on through the park and up the short, paved hill to my co-op apartment. Once inside the gate, Fordham Hills Owners Cooperative complex was like being in another world within the Bronx borough. There were well-groomed trees that blossomed in the spring and finely maintained grounds of grass and annual flowers where squirrels bounced and birds flew. The location was an urban oasis. It took years of friendships and acquaintances and seeing where and how they lived in the City for me to understand that living on The Hill in the Bronx off Sedgwick Avenue and Fordham Road was a distinction. In realizing this, I never ever thought I was better than anyone else— just differently blessed. I was blessed to have home ownership in a comfortable one bedroom—I had moved from the studio apartment by then—on the top floor in one of seven buildings positioned on a circular drive. Of course, Bennett knew where I lived. He also knew I was married. He saw me walk through the park and complex gate many times—with Bobby on occasions. We acknowledged each other in passing while he'd people-watch and hum a tune. The scenario happened often, and I started to wonder if it was intentional.

One weekend, my mother was visiting with me, and we had spent the day shopping. By this time, Bobby had made his 'I do not want to be married anymore' announcement and moved back to the west coast. On the walk to my apartment after shopping, Mommy and I came upon Bennett in the usual spot. We stopped, and I introduced her. My mother is a singer and recognizes a good voice and music when she hears it. She was impressed with Bennett. After introductions, the two chatted a little about their hopes, dreams, and experiences in the music industry. By the time they finished chatting, Bennett had invited my mother and me to a jazz brunch the next day.

Sunday brunches in Manhattan were special. It was especially nice to be with my mother and this familiar acquaintance, hearing his friends play at a cozy restaurant on 86th and Columbus. It was a delightful, early-afternoon New York City experience. All-you-can-eat, made to order crepes and hash browns, with mimosas to wash down the faire, were the order of the day. The company, the entertainment, and the meal were all delicious. We laughed and joked as the food kept coming and the drinks flowed as ordered. My mother really enjoys buffets and all-you-can-eat food bars on top of great music. I know she was having a marvelous time. By the end of the occasion, I felt Mommy really liked Bennett for me, even though I was not of that mindset, yet.

A marital separation with imminent divorce and intense undergraduate studies were occurring for me when I saw Bennett on the elevated platform. I had not seen him at all in the two years since the early-afternoon delightful jazz brunch, nor had we exchanged numbers to keep in touch. I thought him a fondly remembered acquaintance from my past until that day-off Saturday afternoon on my way to SoHo. We were happy to see one another and shouted greetings. His train arrived. He boarded and walked across the car to nod good bye though the door window. Coincidentally—for sure—I saw him again later that day, upon returning from SoHo, as he headed down the stairs from the opposite platform.

"Hey. It's Carol, right?" He approached me with calm enthusiasm.

"That's right. Bennett?" I responded, pretending to not be 100% sure of his name, yet equally calm and enthusiastic to see him.

"Yes! You remember!" He cheered with a bashful smirk and nudged me. Two years of rock-hard, silent ice broke that quickly. We walked the three blocks together towards the park, recovering lost time and recalling moments past when we had seen each other. I wanted to see him again and stay connected, so I gave him my number and asked for his. Now, there would be no excuse not to stay in touch.

2577 Sherman Avenue

My days and nights spent in classes at Marymount Manhattan College, in the studios there painting and drawing, or in galleries and museums reviewing and writing about art—I was majoring in studio art and taking art history courses—were wonderful but very predictable. After papers and tests were marked with high grades and accolades from professors, it was time to go home and be greeted by my two cuddly cats. The pets were of great comfort, and I truly appreciated their attention, but I wanted the warmth and affection only a man could bring. Bold and confident, I retrieved the paper with Bennett's number and called him. I had no plan in mind other than to see him, laugh, and spend time together. I figured he could play his music, sing some of his songs and take my mind away from the fact that I had not been with a man in the year since Bobby and I had separated. As a one-man woman who absolutely loves to be loved and who does not sleep around, my patience was wearing thin, and my desire for human affection was ever-increasing. I sensed something similar in Bennett, and I felt safe with him. I had seen him with a woman only once, years earlier. He had introduced her as his fiancée. That was around the time Bennett and I had first met. Since he did not appear to be involved with anyone now, I felt it okay to give him a call and spend time together. We could be non-physical platonic friends, and my lonesomeness would be put at bay, satisfied with having male companionship.

During the call, we comfortably chatted and joked just as I had anticipated. Bennett invited me to his apartment to watch him play and listen as he recorded his latest songs. I was excited for the change of pace and enthusiastically ventured beyond my iron-gated community and up his long, unfamiliar block of double-parked cars. Upon entering 2577 Sherman Avenue and passing through the once beautifully ornate art deco foyer of the building, I had to go up three worn mahogany-trimmed steps to the lobby and elevator. Where my building elevators were Pine Sol clean, his stank of urine. I would not be surprised to hear Bennett confess today that he wanted me to make the journey solo from my apartment to his, so I could see his world for the first time without him present, distracting, or protecting.

The early summer evening still shown daylight when I fearlessly walked to 2577 Sherman Avenue for the first time. I made the trip on foot in five minutes, rang the buzzer, went up the elevator, and coolly rang his doorbell. "You made it!" Bennett opened the door appearing surprised, yet excited, with a hint of a "Are you okay?" look on his face. He invited me in. Upon entering, I noticed that directly across from his front door was a closed door. He later told me it was his sister's room—she had moved out by then. The long hall to the immediate left led to the living room and dining room. I followed him there. He offered me a seat on the couch and asked if I wanted anything to drink.

"No thank you. I am fine," I said.

"Okay. I will be right back," he said, leaving the room. I sat perusing the place, taking in the atmosphere and décor.

Bennett lived with his widowed mother, and it showed. The outdated couch still had its store-new, thick plastic cover. The waxed dark-wood dining room table had curved legs with ball feet, and the chairs had yellow faux-velvet-covered seat cushions. On the wall was a set of kitsch black velvet art of children with large, sad eyes and balloons. It was not my taste, but it was kind of comforting to see the furniture and art in this unpretentious household. The room was dimly lit except for a bright lamp shining on top of an upright piano against the wall. There was a wall-mounted, framed mirror above the piano. The mirror was tilted slightly inward, so anyone playing could see their reflection and those sitting on the couch as well as those entering or standing in the room. Bennett's surroundings were not well off, but he was living happy with his mother and making his music—circumstances money could not buy. Wealth is wonderful, and I am completely welcome and receptive to it, but for me love outweighs everything, and I decided right then and there I could learn to love Bennett and be happy in his world.

Piano Man

Bennett was not gone long. He returned carrying a pitcher of lemonade and two glasses on a tray. "I brought you a glass in case you change your mind." He placed the tray on the dining room table, poured a glass of lemonade for himself and walked over to the piano. "Relax. Don't be a stiff. Pull up a chair," he jokingly ordered and motioned to me, then placed his glass of lemonade on a TV tray next to the piano and sat on the bench. "I want to play my latest song for you." Bennett turned, and saw I had not moved, and pulled up a chair so I could sit down. I got up and sat diagonally behind him and could see his reflection in the low-mounted mirror. Bennett went from seeing me, to looking at his own image, to closing his dark-brown, piercing eyes as he played the opening chords of a sultry-smooth melody. He sang soothingly, as if he were consoling a child turned woman:

Don't be sad that you broke your china doll.
That you can mend.
If your heart is ever shattered,
Come to me.
To it I will attend.

The lyrics were sung by a man who clearly knew about heartbreak and had confident compassion to heal. I so enjoyed his passion for music. There was no doubt in that moment I would one day love Bennett.

He played and sang several of his songs that night and a few familiar tunes he uniquely re-rendered. Hours passed. It was two o'clock in the morning and time for me to return home to The Hill. I knew it best to go and reluctantly got ready to leave while he found and put on his jacket to escort me home. The only thing keeping me from staying that night was my conscience. It was already the next day, but neither one of us gave indication that me staying and us sleeping together was what we wanted. It was far too soon, and we were just getting to know each other, though we had known each other in passing for nearly three years.

Bennett was comforted by my going to his world. He saw I was grounded and level headed and that I could hang with him without pretense. More than ever before, it was important for me to be my true self. I wanted to be with him, so it was important to just simply be me. I had travelled to other continents and countries, performed in the presence of dignitaries, dined with dance royalty, and touched natural wonders of the world, but with this man I laughed louder and smiled brighter than the joy any of those circumstances had brought. I decided I wanted to be with Bennett. I wanted to know him better. I wanted to grow with him. He trusted me and did not hesitate to reveal his true self, nor was I hesitant to expose the real me.

Over the course of three months after my first visit to Bennett's home, we had many more night adventures. It worked for us to meet late as I did not get home from school activities until eleven, and he was a night owl, most prolific after ten. Our time together became more and more comfortable. We evolved from passing greetings at the park, to me making night visits to his apartment to hear music and enjoy a serenade or two, to talking on the phone on nights that I stayed home. While our departures soon included a goodbye kiss on the cheek, both of us were starting to want more.

One Friday night when Bennett and I were together after my eight-hour day of class and studies, our late-night music review turned into an early morning of watching television in his room on his bed. We kissed more intimately and took off clothes. I was disrobed to a leopard-print teddy, and he to his boxers, when he excused himself and returned with two warm, wet wash cloths. Without saying a word Bennett began to carefully wipe my body clean from the day's dirt and grime. Then he did the same to himself. I had never known of a man to do anything like that. The refreshing care was very comforting. It was reassuring to know we were both wiped clean before choosing to engage in more intimacy. Bennett was thoroughly attentive and careful not to cause discomfort when expressing the depths of his passion for and to me. The feelings we shared were a complete and true adult adoration. Not only did we adore each other, we grew to be in love. We connected and felt each other in ways that reached our highest physical sensibilities. Bennett instinctively knew how to lead and direct me, and I was so wanting and very willing to follow. With Bennett I discovered what it meant—as an adult—to be in love with someone. Such knowledge commenced when we experienced complete care and surrender that night for the first time.

On the next early Saturday afternoon after our late night-into-morning time of passionate, caring love, we made and ate a home-cooked pancakes, eggs, and orange juice brunch. When we were full and satisfied, we went out and walked a few blocks from his home to the nearby Bronx Community College. An inviting bench on the campus called our names that lazy, bright Saturday. He led me to the bench and lay down, then guided me to lie on top of him. We fell asleep almost immediately, with him holding me tight and our hearts beating in sync. About an hour went by, though it seemed like the entire day had passed, until we were awakened by a security officer whistling nearby and students in the distance laughing while playing Frisbee. I was in complete, perfect bliss in Bennett's arms. I did not want to get up but began to move.

He held me a little tighter and said, "Hey." When Bennett saw I was fully conscious, he kissed my forehead. I lifted my head and kissed his lips, then closed my eyes and rested my head back down on his chest. The sound of birds chirping and happy people filled the air. "I love you," Bennett said.

"I love you, too." I raised up to open my eyes and looked into his.

"I am in love with you, Carol." The words flowed with confidence and ease.

Wow! Is what I thought. My heartfelt response was that I was in love with Bennett, and I went on to tell him as much. Bennett laughed in delight, hugged me tighter, and said, "Good. That's really good." Then he kissed me again.

Overcoat and Stilettos

Some may think the title "Overcoat and Stilettos" sounds like a day of streetwalking, but for this woman who was once a small-town girl, who had spent summer vacations at Saratoga Race Course with her maternal grandparents, the segment title brings to mind a day at the horse races where the horses all seemed to be named for inanimate concepts, like "Dream Catcher" and "Kodak Moment." Neither streetwalking nor a day at the horse races is what I write about, though some may question the former thought after reading. Instead, I will talk about a night when my heart raced as I sprinted in heels to Bennett's place.

Bennett and I often performed unexpected acts of endearment for each other. We competed to see who could outdo the other with a fun surprise. He had called me down one fall night to find him at the park fence in a like-new Honda Civic. Once out the gate, I saw lights flash and heard his pet name for me: "Smooch!" Bennett was in the driver's seat, calling to me. I realized it was him, let out a screech, and went running. He had inherited the vehicle from a recently deceased relative. I jumped in the passenger seat, and we went off for a night's drive through the neighborhood.

Weeks later, it was my turn to excite him with a surprise. Remember, I am a woman who loves to be loved. Bennett had an ability to share love like none other, so I wanted to give him a surprise that would entice him to love me like never before. What to do? I searched my closet, found an oversized vintage overcoat, and had the answer. The idea was not original, though. I intended to do what one of my former DTH colleagues once told me she had done for her boyfriend. I showered, got dolled up, put on the heels and overcoat, and raced to Bennett's. It was a cold night. I ran to generate heat, as well as, to get to his apartment as fast as I could—but I had to clear five metaphoric hurdles on the way to the finish line.

The first hurdle was to walk swiftly down the hill and pass the security guard. The guard was cordial as always and wished me a good evening before unlocking the gate. I wished him a happy night in return and galloped off the cooperative grounds. The first hurdle was cleared. I held the wrapped overcoat tightly to prevent any breeze from creeping through. I was sweating with nervous excitement, and my pores were open. Staying tightly covered was necessary to prevent the crisp air from touching me and to avoid catching a cold.

Prancing through the park was the next hurdle. I did not want to look suspicious and call unwanted attention to myself, so I nodded and smiled while passing the familiar men sitting in the park holding small brown paper bags covering cans of 'soda.' The walking-through-the-park hurdle was quickly cleared, with a huge sigh of relief that I had not tripped or fallen. I halted at the stoplight outside the park fence and stood at the curb, waiting for the traffic light to change. A lot of people were out that night. The cold air did not keep them from making a night's run to the corner convenience store or up a block to get a slice of pizza. I had stood at that light many times before, but it seemed extra-long that night, and all eyes seemed to be looking at me. I released the feelings of paranoia just as the light changed, and crossed the street.

With the second hurdle behind me, there were only three more to go. Dashing up the long block to Bennett's apartment building was an easy, uneventful hurdle to clear. I called Bennett before leaving home to make sure he'd be there. He did not ask who it was when I rang the intercom, and he buzzed me right in. There wasn't a soul in the entrance foyer or lobby—the next to last hurdle to clear. I made it to the elevator—the final hurdle. The elevator made five stops before it reached the ground level. Almost every one of the seven people who exited checked out my legs, ankles, and high heels. Some looked at my face first. I maintained eye contact and smiled at those who did to distract them from glimpsing at the rest of me.

When everyone got off the elevator, I got on. Bennett lived on the ninth floor. The elevator stopped at floors three, four, six, and seven on the way up. The people who got on were willing to go up in order to be in an elevator and eventually go down because the other elevator was out of order. We finally reached the ninth floor, and the door opened. I exited immediately. Every eye was certainly on me, as I could feel them watching me in my hind-sight. The elevator doors were still open when I walked to Bennett's door directly across from the elevator. I rang his bell, and he immediately opened the door. Just as the elevator doors were closing, Bennett gave a smirk and a nod to one of the passengers. I abruptly turned and saw a male passenger hold his thumb up, wink, and smile.

The last hurdle was crossed, and I had made it past the finish line. Once over the threshold and inside his apartment, I closed the door, and BAAM, flung the oversized overcoat open to reveal my sculpted-dancer physique, with legs and feet in silver stiletto, high-heeled pumps. I was dressed for a surprise private party for Bennett and me! He gasped in delight, with wide eyes. He laughed and motioned 'shush,' then quickly grabbed me to rewrap my coat. His mother was down the hall in the kitchen. As attractive as I appeared, he would not chance her seeing me. I completely agreed and helped by tightly holding the coat closed. The pleasurable sight of me was for his eyes only.

We headed down the hall towards his bedroom, passing the kitchen first. I saw Bennett's mother and stopped, still holding my coat tightly closed. She was sitting in her usual spot at the kitchen table. "Hi, Mrs. James," I said waving to her through the doorway as Bennett passed me and walked in.

"Good evening, Carol. I see you have on your heavy coat. It must be pretty cold out by now."

"Yes ma'am, it is," I responded as poised as possible, feeling like she knew exactly what I had on, especially upon seeing my ankles and bare feet in shoes. Bennett closed the refrigerator door and headed towards me empty-handed. I figured he went into the kitchen to get a view of me from his mother's perspective to make sure I was covered.

"Come on. I want to show you something." He headed towards me, passed me, and walked to his room.

"Okay." I turned to him, then back to his mother. "See you later, Mrs. James." I waved goodbye and followed Bennett to his room.

Bennett shut the door after I walked in. He came up behind me and reached over the shoulders, grabbed the coat, lifted it up, and slid it down my back and off my arms. With the coat draped over his right arm, he walked to my front to study me slowly from head to toe. I wanted him to see every side of me so I held my arms out to the sides, crossed my left foot over my right, and pivoted a slow and steady promenade. After the display, Bennett dropped the coat and reached to grab hold and kiss me.

Being with Bennett helped me to love the physical me. I felt beautiful in my body and looking at my body. I saw my body through his eyes as well. He treated my body like a delicate china doll, to be handled with care. From my time with Bennett, I know how magical physical love can be. I learned the greatest lessons with Bennett of how a man and a woman can all-inclusively love one another. He introduced me to a beautiful love experience that was nurturing and patient. It humbled me to be with a man who cared for me as much as himself. I did not feel a need to direct and lead, pretending to know everything when with Bennett. I willingly was the student and let him teach me. I was hungry and eager for the knowledge and soaked it up. He never rushed a moment of discovering and uncovering the depths of our love. I learned not to rush the unfolding of our love, but to allow each lesson to saturate my being and remain internalized forever, leaving me expecting no less.

Bennett greatly enjoyed the overcoat and stilettos adventure. He reciprocated one night by cleaning my kitchen and having a home-cooked meal prepared when I returned home from long hours of studying. I completely loved his effort. A man who cooks and cleans unexpectedly for me is a huge turn on. What I would decide to do for him next had to be equally domestic, considerate, and stimulating.

Lost Ring and Apple Pie

Bennett often sarcastically joked, asking me if I knew how to cook. Aside from a brunch that we had cooked together at his place, he had yet to see me prepare and eat a meal at home. It's not that I could not cook, for when I did I'd go all out by getting the best and freshest ingredients and following a professional recipe. Years of long hours in the dance studio and theaters, as well as weeks and months on the road performing and living out of a suitcase in hotel rooms with no kitchen, resulted in zero time and practice expressing healthy culinary habits. This was true both during and after my dance career. These circumstances led to poor eating habits and a lack of cooking regularly for my man or for me. So once when I was on break from studies, I showed Bennett I could indeed cook, and added a little surprise fun to it, too.

Life is meant to be lived with abundant joy and excitement. I could not be bored to tears with fretting and frowning, when answering and addressing the meaning of life could bring me much laughter and happiness. I certainly did not live a hum-drum existence during my life with Bennett. Our love inspired me to reach new heights of creative expression that were unpredictable and full of spontaneity. The overcoat and stilettos episode was definitely a spontaneous act. My next surprise would be planned and time-consuming in preparation but so worth the time and effort. I wanted to show Bennett how good of a cook I was and how much fun I could be.

Mother's apple pie was, literally, my favorite. I watched Mommy make them throughout the years and had vivid recollection and sufficient memory of how to make one myself. First, I picked up a bag of baking apples, a pound of sugar, and a box of Jiffy pie crust mix from the supermarket. I had butter, cinnamon, nutmeg and flour at home, completing the required ingredients. Peeling and chopping up the apples is the most tedious step. Twelve medium-size apples is more than enough for a deep-dish pie, so I spiral-sheared the skin off that many. Each curl was a delicious treat to hold me over until the pie was done. I munched and snacked between cutting apple chunks from the core, then polished off the meat until only seeds and transparent pods shown.

I tossed the bare apple chunks in a big bowl, then poured in the right amounts of sugar, cinnamon, nutmeg, and butter. After the filling was stirred to taste just right, it was time to make the crust into a ball as directed. Preparing the bed to flatten out the crust is a sensual part of pie making. It can be the messiest part too. I love pouring flour into a huge heap on the counter and spreading it out with my clean, dry hands. Drawing lines and a face through it, then spreading it out again allows me to enjoy the feeling of the powdery, smooth, soft texture. I was careful not to spread too freely to avoid a spill-over mess on the floor. Cleaning the floor would be too time-consuming, and I needed my minutes to pour the filling, cover the pie, pinch the edges, and bake it. Once baked, it was time to finish staging the surprise.

I called Bennett on the phone and told him to hurry over because I had "lost my ring" in the park near the cooperative grounds' west side entrance. As soon as I hung up the phone, I rushed to the park with the pie neatly wrapped in a shopping bag, then hid it under the park bench. Bennett ran into the park moments after I hid the pie. As soon as I saw him, I prepared to deliver my story with Oscar-worthy drama. I met up with Bennett as he ran towards me and grabbed his arm, pulling and reporting exaggeratedly. "I was sitting on the bench reading and dropped my ring! Help me find it!" Details like when I dropped the ring, why I was in the park at nightfall reading (or if it was daylight when lost), and why I returned after dark to look for it, went unexplained. The questions were not even posed by Bennett. I frantically continued, "It must be under the bench somewhere!" Bennett was a good man-friend and looked around the grass first before going to the bench. Surely he suspected I was up to something.

"Oooo, what is that?" I pointed to the bag, trying not to laugh. He gave me a 'what are you up to now?' look with a smirk, then removed the bag and sat on the bench. I sat next to him and watched him open it. "What is that?" I asked, trying to act like I had no idea. He looked inside and pulled out the slightly softened container of Haagen Daas vanilla bean ice cream, plastic forks, spoons, knives, paper plates, and napkins that I had packed in a large, sealed Ziploc baggie along with the pie. Then he reached in the bag again with both hands and pulled out the warm pie. "Surprise!" I exclaimed, so proudly.

"Smoooooch! What is this?" He smiled bashfully in a confident-man kind of way and sniffed the pie. The spiced apple aroma overrode the pollution and filled the air as he uncovered the pie.

"See, I can cook!" I announced with more pride, feeling especially happy because I baked it for my man and he was pleased.

In Between the Moon and New York City

Physical love was the way Bennett and I most brilliantly communicated. Discovering new ways and exploring uncharted means to express our love were rewarding adventures. We shared love on my cooperative building rooftop. We shared love on the living-room carpet at my parent's house in Poughkeepsie. Key words to contemplate here are "we shared love," which are quite different from "we had sex." The latter was part of our relationship, but sharing love for us was all-encompassing and extended beyond our acts of physical intimacy. We evolved to know how to perceive and respond to one another's feelings and desires. The lyrics from a popular 1980s song fittingly describe the evolution of one special night of spontaneity that Bennett and I enjoyed with no regard for rules, regulations or laws—"When you get lost between the moon and New York City, the best that you can do is fall in love." The lyrics are from the theme song sung by Christopher Cross for the movie *Arthur*. We certainly got caught up in and between the moon and New York City one night, to the point where nothing could have passed between us if it tried.

The night of Bennett and my rooftop rendezvous began in my bedroom on the top floor of Essex building #7 in cooperative apartment #17E of Fordham Hills Owners Cooperative Apartments. Indicative of a romantic story setting, it was a beautiful starry night—a common theme in my love life: stars-night-moon-roof. The moon light shown bright through my bedroom window, and Bennett and I decided to grab a blanket and venture one flight up to the roof to view the entire sky. The roof area was off limits to residents of the building, so we had it all to ourselves. Bennett and I walked around the roof near the low-walled edge for a panoramic view of the Bronx borough and some of Manhattan too.

When we made our way back to the roof entrance door, we picked a spot nearby, spread out the blanket, and lay down on our backs to gaze at the stars and moon. The setting could not have been more romantic. Before long we went from lying side by side discussing the Dippers and

Hercules constellations, to Bennett on top of me. As we touched lips and kissed, we gave and received breath from one another. It was our way of giving the greatest gift—the breath of life. He would blow breath into me. I would capture it, draw and swallow it in, then reciprocate to him. Such exchanges were commonplace, metaphorically making our intimacies a nurturing and life-sustaining experience.

From the rooftop, Bennett and I gave more breathtaking life as we had shared precious love at my childhood home. Some relatives and friends had come to Poughkeepsie for my college graduation party. Before nightfall most of the friends and relatives had gone home, and my aunt, a cousin, and Bennett remained to spend the night. There were three bedrooms in the house—one bedroom for my parents, one bedroom that use to be Chy's—Chy had left home, married, and was a mother, by then—and one bedroom for me. Aunt Sally was sleeping in Chy's old room. Once Cousin Kim fell asleep in the bed next to me, I got up to go see Bennett, who was lying on the floor in a sleeping bag in the living room.

When I appeared, Bennett unzipped the bag to make room for me to lie by his side. I did not want to waste time talking and went right to lie on top of him. He pulled back and pushed me away with a look and motion of "What are you doing? Your parents are in the room right there!" I shrugged and continued, and almost instantly it was okay with Bennett, who helped by pulling me to him. We immediately began acting on the expressions of our love. It was ever more delicious because my parents were only a closed door away and possibly asleep. Bennett and I were adults, well over twenty-five, and we were in love, without a care or worry of anyone to disapprove. We were humans—in our case, a woman and a man—drawn to do what humans do when in love. In our humanness, we were free and uninhibited, sharing our close connection, giving each other breaths of life.

After my and Bennett's night time together in the living room in Poughkeepsie, I eventually returned to my room to get some rest. The entire household awakened after dawn. Mommy, Daddy, Aunt Sally, Kim, Bennett, and I had breakfast. Soon after eating, all of us, except my parents, left to return to our homes in New York City. During the entire train ride on the way back to my apartment, there was one question I contemplated asking Bennett. He and I had been discussing going into business together and opening a fine arts school, where he'd teach and run the music department, and I'd teach and direct the dance division. We even went as far as to view available real estate in New York City to possibly house the arts institution. If we were going to create such an establishment together, I needed to be assured I could trust Bennett to partner with me in owning a fine arts business, which was my life's dream. Essentially, I needed to know I could trust Bennett with my life. So, I decided to ask him to marry me.

The Proposal

Bennett and my surroundings were always simple. Some may say they were outright poor. That did not matter to me, though, for our love was all the wealth I desired. Our love was more than plentiful. It nourished and strengthened my spirit daily. I felt as long as we had each other, life would work itself out.

After returning from Poughkeepsie, Bennett picked me up at about eight o'clock for one of our evening neighborhood drives to the local Chinese food take-out restaurant. General Tso's chicken was our favorite dish to order. It was so sweet, succulent, and filling on top of white or fried rice. The dark-red color of the 'chicken' left the origin of the meat suspect, though. Still, the food was delicious, masked in caramel-colored sauce and breading sprinkled with sesame seeds. Bennett was waiting for me in the car by the park fence when I walked out the complex gate. I chassed to the driver's side, opened the door, and threw my left leg over to his other side to sit straddled, facing him. With arms wrapped around his neck, I gave him a huge kiss on the lips, pulled back, looked him straight in the eyes and said, "I love you, Bennett. Will you marry me?"

He pulled back and gave me a 'What did you say?' look with an inquisitive brow and partial smirk, but no answer. Then he proceeded to pick me off of him and maneuvered me to sit in the front passenger seat. Bennett may have thought I was playing, but I was dead serious and would have followed through if he had said yes. Nothing was said, though. Because nothing was said that evening or over the days, weeks, and months that followed my proposal, I decided not to bring it up again and reasoned that it was time to take steps to begin anew.

I believed I could live with Bennett in contented bliss and always figure out ways to keep us there because that is how I strive to live life, and because I loved him so much. Our love was all I believed I needed to live happily ever after. Truth is, I was an aggressive go-getter when compared to his complacent spirit, and the romance may have worn off. I probably would have gotten tired of the roach-spray smell in the apartment and in our clothes. I know I would always long for a dream life in a dream house with flowers in window boxes and a white picket fence out front. That was not Bennett's immediate desire. He was emotionally invested in New York City. He loved his music-life there, and had endless fantasies of what to do with it. I would not stick around to experience our love crumble. Instead, four months post-graduation from Marymount Manhattan College, with a degree in-hand, I left New York one fall's-beginning with seven suitcases and my two cats. I was heading for a job in Virginia with a supportive community that would nurture my professional expertise and help me establish a life that could bring me the house of my dreams with flower boxes and fence.

MMC Graduation, June 1991

SCENE 3

Specious

spe·cious [spee-shuh s] adjective;

1. apparently good or right though lacking real merit
2. pleasing to the eye but deceptive

"Because I desired to learn all I could about love, specious-love was an inevitable love for me to experience, and when I did, it was a long and hard lesson to learn."

THERE ISN'T A MORE APPROPRIATE word to describe the situation, my life with him, and the man himself. He looked and seemed good and right. He was pleasing to the eye and presented a believable story at first, especially because I wanted to be in love. He seemed to be an ideal man who said and did all the right things. I felt comfortable sharing my desires, my dreams, my secrets, and myself with him. I trusted him, though I'd known him only a short time before we married—ten months, to be exact. I wanted to believe God had brought a knight in shining armor to rescue me from singlehood, childlessness, and being dream-house deprived. He cast the line and hungry obsessed me nibbled, grabbed the bait, and was caught up in a life of deception.

I was unfamiliar with the word 'specious' but saw it as the perfect title for this scene after receiving the following, unsolicited message via email:

Carol,

When you have said to me for years, 'If you set one foot on my property, I'll call the police and have you arrested for trespassing,' your specious well wishes are met with skepticism.

When you try to berate me in front of Hunter and Garland, your specious well wishes are met with skepticism.

When I provided a roof over your head (and Hunter and Garland's), and then you in collaboration with your mother bought the first house on Ardmore (without consulting me and without my knowledge) and tried to take Hunter and Garland, then cried foul when others sincerely asked you your reason for leaving, your specious well wishes are met with skepticism.

When you engage in fait accompli your specious well wishes are met with skepticism [fait accompli (fe za-kawn-**plee)** French. 1. an accomplished fact; a thing already done].

When you allow under age children to consume alcohol and drugs and try to cover it up, and allow them to engage in sex at Ardmore, your specious well wishes are met with skepticism.

When you schedule Hunter and Garland's appointments and extracurricular activities on my visitation time, your specious well wishes are met with skepticism.

When I have been required to pay court-ordered child support ($876.00 per month) to the Department of Child Support Services that eventually is deposited into your banking account, and you tell others that I have not paid you a cent in Child Support, your specious well wishes are met with skepticism.

When you have not thanked me for providing $45,000.00 for the initial renovations of the dance studio, your specious well wishes are met with skepticism.

When you intentionally do not either place my name with the studio, or acknowledge my contribution, your specious well wishes are met with skepticism.

When I was there through your initial Multiple Sclerosis diagnosis and you tell me and others that the only MS that you have is me, your specious well wishes are met with skepticism.

When I know you tell Hunter and Garland not to engage in certain behavior, and you engage in that same behavior, your hypocrisy stands out, and, your specious well wishes are met with skepticism.

Now, I cannot tell you what to do, or how to conduct your life, but it remains, your specious well wishes are met with skepticism.

A word to you, Hunter and Garland have confided in me about you, and we have a completely different perception of you, which is far from what you wrote, "I am and always have been a nice and loving woman."

Get real, get serious, it is your soul.

Chester

Phew! What a bizarre trip! The man's mind worked in ways that were unreal and incomprehensible. The majority of what he wrote was false and misconstrued interpretations, to say the least. It was fruitless to argue and take defense—no one ever won arguing with him. However, one point he wrote was true. I forbid him from coming on my property without my permission. He became too scary and unpredictable. There was no telling what he would do out of jealousy and resentment. I made a huge error in judgment when it came to him, but our union was worth the turmoil, for it gave the world my two children, Hunter and Garland, and I'd do it all over again to have them in my life.

I did a lot of character-searching to write about this love-lesson, mainly because I did not wish to hurt my family, his family, or him—or me! I believe, however, challenging situations—human phenomena from relationships to illness—are presented because a loving heart and mind can overcome them and live to tell the story to benefit humankind. So here, I share my experience with love and the intention to strengthen and inspire all readers.

New Beginning

By October 3, 1991 I had packed, moved from New York City, and was settling into an apartment in Blacksburg, Virginia. The carpeted one bedroom was clean and plain with electricity, running water, a kitchen and a bathroom. The place provided privacy and a roof over my head. I was able to expand my boundaries and view a bit of the countryside by crossing the threshold of the sliding glass door and stepping out onto the balcony. It was my place of residence, but not home. I wanted to attach flower boxes to the balcony rail or the apartment windows to add blooming color to the surroundings, but it was not allowed. So, I almost immediately began searching for affordable real estate to buy and ultimately affix my stamp of beauty. The houses that fit my budget were twenty to forty-five minutes away from work in the next town or in adjacent counties, and I did not have a car. Besides, it was not advisable for a single woman to live by herself in the isolated locations where some of the houses stood. I know I can be stubbornly determined to get what I want and what feels right for me, but I also know I can jump into situations without considering all the facts and heeding the warning signs. Fortunately, I did not contract to buy any of the affordable houses I viewed in the early days of my transition, as life had truly shown me it pays to wait.

In November, my parents came to visit and celebrate Thanksgiving with me. The apartment was not the most festive environment, so we went out to eat. Such happenstance added to my determination to own my own home. It was emotionally and psychologically important for me to have a place to call my own, to invite friends and family over for dinners and such, and to continuously improve and grow in equity and wealth. I was too bright of a woman, and I had worked too hard and well to earn what I achieved, not to realize that dream. December came, winter break was near, and I still had not bought a house. Was I so obsessed and determined to buy a house—to own 'this thing' that I would negate love? The answer is yes: I wanted a home partly to house my ideal family, a piece still needed to complete my life's puzzle. But the answer is also no: I had not given up on love, or at least not on the idea of it.

Love had many phases for me. I had experienced tender, sweet childhood love with Aaron and sharing, adult love with Bennett. Because of these two men, my expectations of love were high, though none of my loves had been permanent in the 'and they lived happily ever after' sense. Love was beautiful and something I believed in without doubt. Because I desired to learn all I could about love, specious-love was an inevitable love for me to experience, and when I did, it was a long and hard lesson to learn.

First Impression at Winter Break

Pleasing sights and scents of the season filled the environment and air. Menorahs and Kinaras lit with burning candles sat on mantles and tabletops to respectively celebrate the Hannakah and Kwanzaa holidays. Mistletoe hung above my workplace threshold for all who entered to see and kiss someone if they chose. I had nobody in mind to kiss, but the idea was pleasant, and it was enjoyable to watch when others acted on the cultural kissing tradition. The last day before break came, and students began heading home for four weeks off. I had not accumulated enough annual leave to go away for the holiday, so I stayed in hopes of catching up on office work while everyone was away. Unfortunately, I learned that the entire Squires Student Center building at Virginia Tech, where my office was located, would be closed for two weeks, so doing office work over break was not possible. A colleague in the student affairs department knew I would be staying in town over break and invited me to have Christmas dinner with her and her family. Because I still did not have a car, her son came to pick me up.

The doorbell rang. I asked who it was, peeked through the door hole and saw a pleasant-looking face with a small mustache and kind smile. I opened the door to let him in and kept it open. In full view, he looked like a Marlboro (cigarette) man, and smelled like one, too. His presence was rustic and included a long-sleeve blue collar shirt, trucker cap, slightly high-water blue dungarees, black sneakers, and a blue down jacket vest. By his unclear eyes and large-pored complexion, I could tell he smoked. "Howdy."—*Oh my gosh*—He talked like a Marlboro man, too!

"Hi. Chester, is it? It is nice to meet you. I'm Carol." I offered my hand to shake, then got my coat, put it on, and headed towards the door.

"You go first." He stood at the door and motioned the path to leave. We stepped out, and he passed me after closing the door for me to lock it.

He was chivalrous, kind, and charming and kept intelligent conversation on the drive to his mother's house a town away. I learned the dinner party would also include his sister, younger brother and girlfriend, and his grandmother. His father was deceased. He had died of a heart attack four years earlier. Since he made a point to say his brother was younger than he, I asked if he had an older brother or other siblings. He had an older brother who was deceased, as well. I asked how his brother had died. He said he'd tell me some other time and changed the subject. I could not help but notice the blackhead deeply embedded on the right side of his face below his sideburn shadow. It was hard not to see, especially because I turned to him often during the drive to carry on pleasant and engaging conversation. He later told me his objective in talking to me during the drive was to find out what was going on in the gray matter between my ears. No doubt I passed with flying colors and even gave more than expected.

The housing development where my colleague lived was adorable. All of the homes were quaint, detached townhouses with guard-railed decks—just right for flower boxes—leading up to the main entrance door. I was in love with her house already and had not yet been inside. Chester pulled the car into the driveway and parked. He got out and dashed to the passenger side to open my door. He was certainly impressive, especially with the way he offered his hand to help me out, and then motioned for me to walk up the deck to the front door. Chester followed, hurriedly passed to open the door, and let me go in first.

Upon entering my colleague's house, the aromas of Christmas dinner, cookies baking, and a live fir Christmas tree oozing a fresh evergreen scent were heavenly to inhale. There were skylights in the vaulted ceiling that made for a bright, inviting welcome into the great room. The house was decorated beautifully for the season—the Christmas tree was adorned in white lights and draped with popcorn garland. My colleague's general eye for interior design was much to be admired. The furniture was tastefully upholstered with a beige and blue sunny California-like fabric, featuring cranes and bamboo. The homey atmosphere and cozy feeling instantly received upon entering her home, and the fact that I adored my colleague, led me to take a more interested look at her son to determine if he was worth getting to know better. I pondered the stats learned on the drive over. Chester came from a highly educated family. His mother had a PhD and taught counseling psychology at Virginia Tech. Her late husband, Chester's father, was a retired attorney. The sister worked for the federal government in international affairs, and the surviving brother had earned a juris doctorate. The family sounded very impressive, yet I never understood exactly what Chester did.

Chester and I exchanged telephone numbers when he drove me home after Christmas dinner. I got to know him better over time, during long-distance phone calls while he was living with his paternal grandmother in Washington, D. C. He said he worked a temp job doing budget management and financial planning at his alma mater and had a bachelor's degree in finance. From the stories he told me about years of tending to family crises and obligations, he had never achieved long-term employment or a career. I gathered from the vague family history Chester shared that his increased familial obligations started when his father became increasingly disabled with a muscular disease. Around that same time, his older brother was diagnosed as manic depressive after he had threatened to harm the family and himself. Chester stepped in a number of times to combat his brother's attacks on the family, and that made things worse. His mother thought it best for Chester not to be around and asked him to move out of the house. Though not living at home anymore, Chester assumed a fatherly role with his younger brother by playing ball with him and doing whatever else his father was not physically capable of doing anymore. The sister, at the time of the outbreak of the older brother's mental illness—which led to dysfunction in the family—was in high school and had left the country to study abroad in the Netherlands as a foreign exchange student. The older brother, in the meantime, could not control his illness and committed suicide. It sounded like while everyone else in the family was living their lives best they could, Chester picked up the slack and forfeited his goals.

Chester lived with his grandmother in D. C. to honor a promise to his father to take care of her, since his father's brother, her primary caretaker, had passed and his father was not physically able to take on the duty. It made sense that Chester's work was temporary because he also had to travel often to his parents' home to help his mom with his dad. I felt sorry for Chester, and the more I was told by him, the more clearly I saw him as a true hero who had sacrificed his life for his family. I also understood why he was not married and had no children. It seemed like there was never time for him to have a personal life and build his own family. Chester deserved a break in life and something good to happen for him. When he was ready, I was willing to make that goodness me.

The Courtship

Chester was a charmer, and in little time he became my Prince Charming. From Christmas dinner through January into February, our daily telephone calls led to weekend visits to see me in Blacksburg. He'd drive down from Washington, D. C. in his yellow Volkswagen Bug—a make, model, and color I liked a lot. I'd see him pull up and park across the street from my workplace; the Black Cultural Center at Virginia Tech (BCC). He'd hop out of the car with flowers in hand and dash into the building. He always entered with great enthusiasm. A huge smile would appear on his face when he saw me. It was adorable.

"These are for you, my dear." Chester would hand the bouquet of flowers to me.

"Oh, these are beautiful! Thank you." I'd take the flowers, sniff them, and go to the storage closet to get a vase. As Chester made routine visits, the students who milled around in and out of the BCC got to know him better. The frequent student visitors came to care a great deal for me. They were my eyes, ears, and pseudo-protectors. They would scrutinize Chester from head to toe, checking out his clothes and appearance, and talk about their opinions of him amongst each other. They'd never tell me their thoughts, though, because they respected and cared for me and did not want to hurt my feelings. If they had told me then that they thought him harsh, rash, and a shyster, I would not have believed it nor wanted to hear it. All I saw and wanted to see was his charm, as well as the thoughtful and sacrificial acts he did for me and his family. All I wanted to see was that he liked me and I liked him, and that the attraction could eventually turn into love. I did not take heed to the warning signs, such as that he did not have a steady job or career, he wore high-water jeans, and the heels of his black sneakers were busted and flapped when he walked. I allowed his pleasing looks, charm, and intelligent talking to let me turn a blind eye to the facts that he was not regularly employed and that he smoked and drank disgusting black coffee.

I was an artist from New York who knew how to turn the raw, plain, and unattractive into refined beauty. I'd be Pygmalion and Chester would be my stone. I fantasized that Chester was like a diamond in the rough, and when I was done shaping and buffing him, he would sparkle to fit just right and be cherished and admired forever by me and everyone. If I had known then what I have uncovered about Chester and have since learned, I would have taken heed to the words from *No Man is an Island*, where Thomas Merton wrote, "The beginning of love is to let those we love be perfectly themselves, and not to twist them to fit our own image. Otherwise, we love only the reflection of ourselves we find in them." If I had read and understood Merton's philosophy before electing to sculpt and shine Chester, I might have realized I had seen enough and decided to focus my attention on polishing me.

Polishing the Stone

My father's approval of Chester was important. I do not know exactly why, but it had always been that I would not make an important life decision until I knew his opinion first. It is not that I necessarily asked or sought his direct approval, but my ears were always attuned to his words and thoughts of wisdom and criticism, and my eyes were always keen to his looks, grimaces, smiles, and pouts for anything he did or did not like. After assessing his reaction, I would act according to what I thought would make him happy and keep me at peace. In essence, I allowed my father to control me. Understandably, he had control when I was a child, but I allowed him to continue to exercise control into my forties. So, there I was in my late-twenties, at the start of the Chester saga, awaiting my father's approval.

In February 1992 when my parents came to visit me again in my new town, digs, and job, they also met my new friend and her son Chester, my new beau by then. My colleague invited my parents and me to Sunday brunch at her house. It was a pleasant gathering, and Chester really laid the charm on them. He had my mother and father enchanted, smiling, laughing, and eating out of the palm of his hands. They, like me, were convinced he was the ideal match for me. When I privately showed my father a ring Chester had given me for Valentine's Day, his face lit up, and he hopefully asked, "Is that an engagement ring?" I told him no, but his bright and accepting reaction to the ring was all the approval I needed to full-heartedly take a chance with Chester.

While embarking into new, uncharted territory with Chester, a huge part of my heart was still with Bennett. He and I continued to talk via phone for months after the big move and while things progressed with Chester. I told Chester about Bennett. Though Chester acted like he did not care at first, he later hinted that I should have considered how he felt, knowing I was actively talking to my ex-lover. My guilt-sensitivities eventually kicked in hard, and I stopped speaking with Bennett, giving Chester the green light to move ahead. He moved fast, ignoring the speed limit, and proposed marriage to me in July. I hopped on board for the drag race, and we planned a fall wedding. My parents, especially my father, were thrilled. Bennett was devastated when I told him. He begged me not to marry Chester. Bennett promised to raise the child if I was marrying Chester because I was pregnant with Chester's child, and if I would return to New York and marry him. I told him no. I did not decide to marry Chester because I was pregnant. I had decided to marry Chester because I loved him. Bennett called my parents crying, telling them how much he still loved me, hoping they would give him comforting words, such as I would go back to him and that I belonged with him. Instead, they told him marrying Chester was what I wanted to do and what was best for me. Sure, I agreed and felt it right and good to marry Chester, but a huge part of my decision was because my father, and, in extension, my mother, were both happy and pleased. Without hesitation or doubt, I would marry Chester at the War Memorial Chapel at Virginia Tech on October 3, 1992—exactly one year after moving to Blacksburg—and in just over three years give my father and mother the grandchildren they longed for, as well as the children I greatly desired to complete my picture of an ideal family.

Rendering the Ideal Family

Almost eleven months after we said, "I do," Hunter Nathanael Smith was born on September 1, 1993. I was 29 years young. Married life and raising Hunter with Chester were wonderful—we were a beautiful family of three. As a new mother, I naturally wanted to be a part of all of the firsts in Hunter's life. So three months after he was born, when my maternity leave was up, Chester and I furnished my office at the Black Cultural Center with a crib to accommodate Hunter occasionally being at work with me.

The Black Cultural Center operated under the auspices of the Dean of Students Office at Virginia Tech when I was the Coordinator for the BCC (October 1991–May 1995). The Assistant Dean and Dean of Students I reported to, as well as the rest of the office, were very supportive of my early maternal needs. Chester found temporary employment at the university by the time Hunter was born and kept a bassinet at his workplace so he could also be a part of Hunter's early life while at work.

As months passed and Hunter grew, keeping him at work was not optimal for him developmentally, nor for Chester or me professionally. So, babysitters were hired to watch him during work hours. I liked my job, but I loved my son, and having someone else taking care of him regularly was bothersome, especially when he made a milestone sans me. Hunter first walked independently at age seven months and seven days young. He was with a babysitter when it happened, and his father and I were at work. When I returned home from work that day, Hunter pitter-pattered briskly to greet me. He had a huge toothless-drool-smile with accentuated dimples in his left cheek and chin. My heart both melted with joy at the sight of him walking and sank in disappointment because I could not share in his triumph sooner. I was present for his first spoken word and when he recognized his first color, though. Hearing him say "bloon, bloon" when he wanted a balloon, and hearing the word "yellow" ringing from his lips when I pointed to a banana and asked, "What color is that?" was music to my ears.

The occasion of Hunter walking and making other monumental developments without me being present made me more determined to restructure my life to support and nurture my growing family and have the experiences I wanted to have with them. The time for this had long past, and it was of the essence to realize my dream. I knew I would have to eventually leave my position at Virginia Tech and pursue owning and operating a dance business, where I could set my own hours and be my own boss while pursuing my passion for dance. I had the determination to open a dance studio long before Hunter was born and found the determination still strongly percolating within me when I was carrying him. At seven months pregnant, I had toured vacant commercial property, but had not signed a lease nor left my full-time job with benefits to start the business. It was not the right time. Such a decision was not practical with a baby on the way, but the determination to open a dance studio soon resurfaced and left me adamant once Hunter was born and he was making great strides.

Beautiful baby Hunter was blessed with loving parents, grandparents, family, and community, all of whom wished the best for him, Chester, and me. To say his grandparents, my parents, Thomas and Elizabeth, loved him dearly would be a gross understatement. They loved him to the moon and back and add to that to infinity and beyond. Grandmother and Grandfather could not do enough for their grandson. His other grandmother, Chester's mother, felt the same and expressly spoke of her first and only known grandchild with so much pride and joy. Whenever Chester's mother was with baby Hunter, she would repeatedly reinforce in his ear and mind that he was handsome and intelligent. Such regular positive suggestion would come to an early end, however. Six weeks before Hunter's first birthday, Chester's mother learned she had colon cancer and received a prognosis of three weeks to live. Life transpired for Chester's mother as predicted, and three weeks to the day after the prognosis, she lay on her deathbed. Chester's mother requested that Hunter lay with her on that day, and Chester and I brought him to her. Chester and I left the room, and I do not know what occurred. I am confident, however, that as a grandmother and her grandson spent their final moments together, the grandmother made it a teaching moment that helped influence Hunter to be the gorgeous and brilliant human being he became.

After Chester's mother passed, Chester received a monetary inheritance, and rather than me taking out a loan, cash was paid to renovate a space leased to house the business. It took about three months to complete the renovation which included one large and one small studio fashioned with sprung floors for safe dance-learning and fun. The Center of Dance was founded in August 1994 at 215 Draper Road, Blacksburg; VA—this was the same location I had toured over a year earlier when pregnant with Hunter. Once renovations were complete and the official ribbon cutting occurred on October 24, 1994, The Center of Dance was in business.

Hunter grew up at the studio. I taught classes with him crawling on the marley—a linoleum-like surface adhered atop the sprung dance floor. He would duck and run under and between dancers' legs that were open in second position, and I would carry him at my hip while demonstrating barre and floor combinations. Life was continuing to be as perfect as desired, if not more so. I had the ideal family and lifestyle, raising my son and running my business simultaneously.

Garland Thomas-Emmanuel Smith was born on December 27, 1995, twenty-seven months after Hunter. He had a well-aware and very alert demeanor from the first time I held him in my arms. I saw and sensed a calm all-knowingness about Garland immediately and got that same feeling from him throughout our days together. Garland was a quiet, watchful, independent, and accommodating child. He would always sit back, watch carefully, and take everything in. If I could not find something—the remote control, for example—all I would have to say—for anyone in earshot to hear—was, "Where's the remote control?" And Garland would quietly walk to the couch and retrieve it from underneath—Garland, like Hunter, was an early walker. He began walking at eight months, eight days young. There were times when Garland was seen one minute and gone the next, then I would hear a strong, prolonged straining grunt coming from an out-of-view corner. Garland had quietly walked to the corner, squatted, and proceeded to push out a bowel movement into his diaper. It was a most darling and adorable act.

It was not long after learning to walk that Garland graduated from diapers to 'big boy' Huggies Pull-Ups—which were essentially the same as diapers for collecting bodily waste. That was still too babyish for one-year-young Garland. If Chester and I insisted that he had to wear Pull-Ups for his comfort and our convenience, Garland was not pleased and rebelled. He would remove the undergarments at night while in bed. After two frustrating months of awakening on a wet mattress, Garland trained himself, with our help, to go to the toilet both night and day. Once he potty-trained, talking came next. Before he could speak, Garland would point and grunt if he wanted something—I once thought that his vocal cords were damaged due to the trauma of meconium being sucked from his throat after birth. Garland spoke his first word, "apple," with a deep, froglike guttural grunt. I was not present when Garland said his first word, because Chester and I were away, but when my parents, who were watching him at the time, put Garland on the phone, and he said, "Hi Mommy and Daddy!" we understood and heard him loud and clear. I thought it was Hunter speaking. "No. That was Garland," Daddy said. Chester and I cheered!

With Hunter and Garland in our lives and a marriage to Chester that appeared wonderful and happy, I felt life could not be more perfect. We had two beautiful children, and proud Chester demonstrated his support for me and fatherly nurturing for the children like a grand public performance. As a performer who enjoyed positive attention, I went along and even promoted the behavior, at first, but circumstances were starting to feel dishonest, unnatural, and fabricated. Chester had a confused way of twisting truth to appear to be the main parent, raising Hunter and Garland while I was operating the studio. Like any good parent would do, Chester would make sure Hunter and Garland were nourished and cared for when I taught or did studio-related work, but I was always there for Hunter and Garland, whether 'free' or not, and I did the majority of the household chores. Chester also claimed to be the breadwinner of the family and the one responsible for my success—both claims coincided with him receiving an inheritance and him controlling how the money was spent. I saw this as a confused state of consciousness because Chester did not have a job when Garland was born, and he would not work.

As for raising Hunter and Garland, it came to a point where I felt the children were controlled like puppets, led and rehearsed for Chester to look good, efficient, and successful. Chester had a lot of knowledge and lived to 'inculcate wisdom'—Chester's words—into the children. Whenever he had the children with him in a public place where there were on-lookers and listeners, the children were drilled—as in this example: "Hunter and Garland, come over here, Misters!" Chester would call the children over in a commanding voice. The children would halt whatever they were doing, jump off a swing or stop a see-saw, leaving another child grounded in the sand, and run to their father. Chester would speak as if continuing the conversation, "Now we rode by a house one day, and there was smoke coming out of a chimney. So I stopped and pointed to it and said, 'What is that; liquid, solid, or gas?'"

That was Hunter's cue to dutifully answer, "Gas."

This would lead into a spiel from Chester about language development that ended with, "So I asked these gentlemen [speaking about the boys], 'Does language shape thought, or does thought shape language?'"

Until about ages six and four, the boys' dictated answer was "Take a few years and think about it." From there on, to age ten for Hunter and age eight for Garland, the answer was "Language and thought are symbiotic." I went along with the display and sometimes thought it was cute, especially when they were younger. As they grew older, however, I saw the children's dislike for this practice. I felt their resentment and embarrassment at being forced to listen to years of rehearsed babble and response on cue with dictated answers. I became tired of the children being controlled like puppets and did not hesitate to make my sentiments known when things did not feel right.

I could no longer play the fool in Chester's court of rule. I was too honest, strong, and capable of a woman to go along with misrepresentations. I could no longer live a lie. When people saw me coming to my senses and seeing Chester for the fake person and shyster he was, my support network came out of the woodwork and turned into an army. They saw I needed help. It was obvious. The stress of Chester not working, the farce I supported, and my being false because I wanted to make things work and appear right with Chester had taken a toll. My body began to malfunction.

I became tired, worn down, and weak, and was diagnosed with multiple sclerosis.

Diagnosed with Multiple Sclerosis

Chester was with me when the disease was diagnosed. "What is multiple sclerosis?" I asked the doctor. "Am I going to die?" My mind went racing with questions, and I wanted comforting answers.

"No," the neurologist responded and laughed. He then proceeded to explain the disease as if reciting a lesson he had memorized from a textbook. I was not impressed with the medical jargon. What I wanted to know was what medicine I could take to get rid of it, not that there was no cure and I had to take interferon injections for the rest of my life, which sounded like a death sentence to me. I got headaches taking vitamins!

After being told the news and internalizing my opinions—which I kept to myself—Chester and I left the doctor's office.

There was thick silence as we walked down the long corridor and out of the hospital without saying a word to one another. Then, when we were out of the building and in the parking lot with no one around, he angrily broke the silence. He repeatedly shouted and ranted, "Now it's my turn to get my life and career in order!" Scared and confused, I wondered why he was so mad at me. I felt guilty, responsible, and incompetent all at once. I felt I had let him down by getting sick. His response and reaction were dumbfounding. He showed no comfort or consolation, but got in his car and drove off in a hurried huff. I was devastated and felt alone, with no idea of what to say or do besides get in my car and drive home.

I turned to God like never before, praying the entire lonely drive home. I asked, then begged, then ultimately pleaded with God to take the symptoms away and make me normal. I began to read the Bible and spiritual publications regularly in search of answers and understanding. God was the One I turned to for comfort, as my mate demonstrated that he neither could nor would be there for me emotionally or physically. Chester would have sex with me infrequently after that day, probably because he knew how much I loved it and wanted to punish me for no longer supporting him publically—he could be that childish and spiteful. As the symptoms progressed, I did not complain or fret about the numbness or discomfort that persisted in my body. Nor would I discuss the diagnosis or my understanding of it. Discussing the situation meant paying it attention and giving it power to exist. I believed if the words multiple sclerosis were not spoken and the concept ignored, it would release, and vanish.

This mindset developed from years of conditioning as a ballet dancer to envision only what's desired and to never complain, show weakness, or admit there was a problem. Even if performing a ballet on pointe with raw, blistered feet, wrenched knees, and Achilles riddled with tendonitis, I learned to remain poised at all times and not allow the audience to see the person behind the character or pain. The delusionary life of the dance artist was ingrained in me. Never once did the characterization of an auto-immune disease infiltrate into my world, and I was determined not to perform the role. Upon being diagnosed, I instantly became a diva, cut rehearsals, and forfeited starring as the victim in the "disease production" of MS. Just as importantly, it was time to stop pretending, as had been the case for ten years that I was in a marriage that was happy, stable, and nurturing when it was everything but that. By me not admitting the reality that had developed over ten years, and by me pretending all was fine and virtually perfect, I was being depleted emotionally, physically, and spiritually. Not to mention, I was not fooling anyone but me.

I decided to be honest about my marital situation and the psychological and emotional abuse I was enduring while married to Chester. I thought through, and owned up to, the order of events that led to the diagnosis. When identified and acknowledged, the culprits, from poor eating, to living with self-imposed stress, to not being true to me and remaining in a marriage turned uncertain with a non-working spouse, had to be worked through and eliminated from my life. I realized I could not blame the diagnosis entirely on Chester, though. He did not make me open the studio and operate it, which was my dream-turned-insistent-choice and was taxing on my physical and mental energy, while raising two small children at the same time. But, I had to do it. Owning and operating a dance studio was the most fitting next step to take on the seamless course of my eternal dance-life.

Path to Eternal Dancing

Here I proceed to reflect on my life as a professional dancer and endeavor to connect how it relates to defining and directing my life at the time of dealing with an uncertain marriage to Chester, raising a family, operating a business and voyaging through a debilitating disease: When my professional career with Dance Theatre of Harlem began in 1978, the stepping stones were laid on my path to eternal dancing. By joining the prestigious Dance Theatre of Harlem, I had subconsciously made a life-long commitment to the art of dance. I will never know where my life would be now and what I would be doing if I did not love dance so much and if I had not been able to realize a livelihood from it. I could not imagine having a better life without the love affair I have had with my life in dance. As a member of DTH I visited places I had only once imagined when seeing them in books. I had never contemplated being outside of the gates of the Garden of Gethsemane, where Biblical history tells us Jesus was found praying and was arrested before his Crucifixion. Yet, that is exactly what I had experienced being with Dance Theatre of Harlem. I wrote in my journal often when on tour with the company to document the life-defining experiences.

> *June 24, 1981: Today, I share more of my experience in Israel. On the way to the Dead Sea on a mandatory culture day, we bravely travelled on a somewhat rickety bus through a desolate terrain. We passed an armored Israeli military vehicle. The troupes were toting machine guns. The land was dry, yet rich in*

spirit and history. Being a visual artist as well as a dancer, I saw the landscape as a blank canvas ready to be colored by my imagination. It may have been a mirage, but I think I saw nomads at a distance herding sheep, and I am "sure" I saw ancient scribes exiting the caves of the Dead Sea Scrolls.

June 27, 1981: Today I share more thoughts of my magical time here in Israel. The performance was in Caesarea tonight at an outdoor amphitheater where the first stone is said to have been laid by Pontius Pilate. The scene was absolutely surreal. Imagine this...Company class and rehearsal are in the early evening when the sun is down and temperatures are cool.

Caesarea, Israel, June 1981

The show started at eleven. We performed the ballet Doina by Royston Maldoom. Doina is a style of Romanian folklore music. The lyrical sound is soothing and longing, bordering on haunting. A pas de deux couple is complimented by six women. Costumes are white form-fitting tubular elastic netting covering the women from head to toe, literally, and the man from neck to ankle. In this cocoon-like garment, dancers transition between curved and angular positions throughout a slow, drawn-out, elongated adagio of music. The story within the movement and music is of the women missing their men who are away at sea. Our audience sat on stone tiers watching as the moon glistened on a backdrop of softly rolling waves of the Mediterranean Sea. It was an incredible, unforgettable experience to dance in that seascape.

Strolling through the corridors of the Hermitage Museum in the former Soviet Union, viewing Byzantine and Renaissance art was not even on my bucket list, but that is what I did one sunny day off in Moscow. Another highlight of my touring days with DTH was performing at the Landestheater in Salzburg, Austria, where the von Trapp family had their final performance in the *Sound of Music* movie. The stone-arched backdrop wall of the stage made for a fun and nostalgic set to run through as I portrayed the Princess of Unreal Beauty in the *Firebird* ballet.

DTH Firebird, 1987

Those tour experiences with DTH began in the late seventies, with eight-hour days six days a week of taking ballet classes and rehearsing in a studio on the second floor of a renovated former fire station. It then turned into a decade-long career of performances in world-famous opera houses, including Covent Garden in London, the Mariinsky Theatre in Saint Petersburg, Russia, the Metropolitan Opera House at Lincoln Center in New York City, and the Kennedy Center for the Performing Arts in Washington, D. C. My career with DTH was phenomenal. It was an unparalleled experience that afforded me the opportunity to be in performances enjoyed by global luminaries such as Her Royal Highness Princess Diana, President and Mrs. Ronald Reagan, Prima Ballerinas Margot Fonteyne and Lynn Seymour, and Danseurs Etoilé Rudolph Nureyev and Mikhail Baryshnikov. I spoke personally with these individuals and learned of their delight to see the performances.

Within all the exterior wonderment, the real joy came from the work and commitment to create a body that was pure pleasure and magic to live in. On a sweltering hot day, we, the Dance Theatre of Harlem dancers, would open the fire escape door to Studio III to catch a breeze of warm summer air. Dancers could be seen in the studio pirouetting in puddles of perspiration without slipping. To successfully turn in such conditions meant realizing the achievement of fine-tuned balance as well as achieving strong muscles for suspension and full body control. Such proficiency was especially useful to me when accomplishing a performance that occurred in the south of France during an arts festival. The arena was an outdoor amphitheater in Arles. It began to rain one evening while we were performing, and freezing temperatures caused the wet stage to ice over, presenting a challenge to dance upon. As the saying goes, "the show must go on," and it did. At the height of the cold-wet-frozen conditions, I had to execute a series of quick and precise double pirouettes on pointe, as if turning on a dime, while dancing as a Russian Girl in George Balanchine's *Serenade.* I depended heavily on the ability to suspend through the torso and lengthen out of the standing leg to successfully complete the series of turns with no break or fall.

This same control developed in years of dance training was relied upon heavily when the multiple sclerosis diagnosis came and muscle weakness began. I once walked in a rhythm and moved to music like nobody's business. Suddenly, movement was cumbersome, stiff, and laborious. Where I once flowed like a willow in the wind and maintained balance for many counts, I remained as stagnant as a block of petrified wood and could no longer stand on my own or upright for even a split second. My dance technique remained strong in my thoughts, however, allowing continued joy through teaching dance in my business. As long as I had strength cognitively and still danced in my mind, no unbalanced marriage filled with confusion and uncertainty would clutter my brain and potentially take away what was left of me to dance. I had to get out of the marriage and establish a stable life. Besides, I would not allow myself to be diminished to a state where Chester would have to take care of me and use the caretaking as an excuse for why he could not work.

Finding a Place of My Own

Stability for me was having a permanent home. As a family, Chester, Hunter, Garland, and I moved to four different places of residence in five years. Two of the residences were rentals, and two of the homes were owned by Chester exclusively. He found one excuse after another as to why my name should not go on the deed. He said that, before putting my name on the deed, my credit needed to be better established, and we should wait for him to accomplish a more credible track record of work because I owned and operated a sole proprietorship. I wanted to be a dutiful wife supporting her husband, so I submitted to his reasoning, though it did not make sense to me. Independent business people own homes all of the time. His reasons for me to not own a home were incomprehensive, but I acquiesced in order to be a "team player," as he admonished me to do time and again.

It was a challenge being on a team with Chester because he was a game changer. As the head of the household, he could not keep permanent employment. He once had a temp job at the university with the potential for full-time employment—that was soon after Hunter was born. I believe he sabotaged his chance for advancement and full-time employment because he did not perform as required and because he kept the baby bassinet at work to accommodate the times he brought Hunter to his office. What at first was a doting father wanting and needing to bond with his newborn, eventually turned into a distraction; for example, when Hunter cried, Chester would pick him up and placed him on his lap, then fed him a bottle while holding a phone to his ear with a shoulder to conduct work-related conversations. When his boss decided to post the position as open for full-time employment, Chester was invited to apply, but the intentions were to hire a more qualified, focused, and capable applicant.

By the time Garland was born, I was focused full-time on developing The Center of Dance and set my schedule around Hunter and Garland's needs and activities. As for expenses, the studio income covered groceries, gas, child care, business expenses, and eventually pre-school tuition. Chester eventually found full-time employment and received comprehensive medical and dental benefits for the family as well as income to pay the household utilities and mortgage—the latter of which I refused to pay because he denied me home ownership. Chester was not happy with his job, though, and soon quit to go back to school for a master's degree in education. That was not my preference for him, for I did not see it in the best interest of the family, but I supported his choice to do better for himself and subsequently for Hunter, Garland, and me—I was still in a confused and uncertain state of mind regarding my marriage and held on to hope for Chester and me and our family.

Upon graduation, Chester began working as a math teacher in an elementary school two towns away. I was elated by this achievement, believing he had found his calling. It was legacy-perfect. His mother, step-grandfather, and uncle were all in education, and now he, with an established life and family responsibilities, had found a fitting career at a later stage in his life. I did not get a chance to fully express my pride in him, though. He was asked to leave the job rather than be fired for insubordination. He managed to charm his way into three more teaching positions after that without having to write "fired" on the applications as the reason for leaving his previous position. He never even told me, his wife, exactly why he lost his positions, but it was always someone else's or the "establishment's" fault. While judging a local arts competition, I ran into one of Chester's former teacher colleagues, and asked why he was let go. She could not disclose specifics of what had happened, but to paraphrase her, she said, "He was telling his co-workers and superiors how to do their job; he had students going home in tears; and he ultimately dug his own grave, jumped in it, and pulled the dirt down to bury himself." I felt somewhat embarrassed, but not at all surprised, and finally had to admit Chester could not be depended upon to keep a job and take care of the children and me.

I do not know why, but hope for Chester and for us continuously crept back into my heart and mind. I remembered why I married Chester and how, although I did not really know him at the time, I had hoped to shape our love and life into an ideal image. The outcome of our union was neither a masterpiece, nor even an aesthetically pleasing illusion, as far as the marriage was concerned. The real picture proved that I had committed to a man who had no idea of who he was, what he wanted, or how to contribute to the world. The unknown of being with Chester was a scary situation to be in and exhausting to circumvent. In hopes of making the marriage work, I had begun to act like him. I did not recognize myself. I began lying and exaggerating to explain his irrational behavior and support my decision to be with him. People saw right through the coloring of his abnormal lens and saw our unhappy marriage. Thank goodness I snapped out of it, for my credibility was also in jeopardy through continued association with Chester. Clearly, it became too risky to be involved with him in a small town where people talk and have defining opinions.

I had a business to run and a reputation to uphold and could not afford to lose clients due to rumors or facts about how Chester unfavorably conducted himself and related to people. When there was a capital campaign to renovate our local theater, he became a member of the steering committee due to his association with me and the dance business. Chester saw it as a position of power and immediately began dictating actions, from fundraising policies to follow to selecting the fabric to upholster the furniture. He was all over the place with advice and had no supporting merit or experience. His modus operandi of frequent opposition led to arguments, and the executive director of the theater threatened to quit. To keep volunteer efforts moving in a positive, unified direction, with no recourse, the steering committee chair asked Chester to resign. I knew the repercussions of these events could tarnish the image of the studio, so as a protective measure, I let him go as my 'extra special assistant.' This was the title he held as a member of the studio team because I did not know what else to call him. He did no accounting, bookkeeping, or filing. He did not answer the phone, and when he greeted people and told them about the business, he was forceful and a turn-off. The whole marriage, the business 'partnership,' and even co-parenting with Chester under one roof had to end, so I once and for all took actions to change things.

Going for drives on a beautiful Sunday afternoon became one of my favorite relaxing pastimes to take my mind off life with Chester. The rides soon expanded into the weekdays, on a mission to find a home. I knew I would never own a house if I remained with Chester, and our family foundation and reputation was eroding before my eyes. Circumstances dictated that I must either sink or swim. My patience was spent, so I told Chester I wanted a divorce and immediately set out to determine how to take care of me, Hunter, and Garland. I had no idea of how to do it, but I had faith that I could. In the process, thoughts of having a debilitating disease remained on the peripherals of my subconscious. They were ignored, though, and I carried on. The constant concern—or disease, if you will—that persisted was the ugly communication and lack of comradeship between Chester and me. It was certainly not good for the children to see, and our discord created anxiety, stress, and unhappiness for all of us. I had definite goals, and Chester was still trying to identify his. In fairness to all, I'd leave him to pursue my dreams on my own, and for him to figure his out on his own, and to give Hunter and Garland stability and a winning chance at life.

Chester knew I could and would accomplish whatever I set my sights on doing and fought me every step of the way. He borrowed a video camera from a church friend and tried to use it to incriminate me. He set it, unbeknownst to me—he thought—and then baited me to argue, so it could be captured on film. He was desperate and thought he was smart, but I was smarter and highly vigilant. I removed the camera when he was not around, then later watched what he had been filming. The clip I saw went from us having a normal conversation in the kitchen to him sitting in the guest bedroom—where I insisted he sleep by then. He was talking into the camera, telling lies about how I abused him and the children. I assumed he was anticipating a legal battle, and I would not let him bare false witness against me without a fight. I immediately started to keep a journal and documented all that was happening daily. In the days and months ahead, his behavior grew more bizarre, desperate, and dangerous, as entered:

- *January 11, 2002 - We argued over how the children should set the table. Chester acted like I was being crazy and demanded the children leave my presence. Hunter did not want to go. Chester dragged Hunter up the hall and into the guest bedroom where Garland already ran. Chester closed the children inside with him, and held the door shut. Hunter and Garland were crying for me. I could not get to them. The door was locked. Things got quiet. Chester opened the door. Hunter and Garland walked out and went to their rooms. There was a heated discussion. I hit Chester over the head with a phonebook. He ran downstairs holding his head and cowering as if hurt. He called someone. I got the children and left. We went to Donald and Jackie's and spent the night. It was cold and the snow was frozen.*
- *March 17, 2002 - We argued. Chester grabbed the children and carried them kicking to the trail behind the house. I got in the car and*

accelerated into the yard. He stopped and let them go.

- April 22, 2002 - I was reading to Hunter in bed. We were under the covers. Chester yanked the blankets off and began filming me and commenting on what I was wearing.
- June 6, 2002 - We argued. Chester led Hunter to the laundry room in the basement and locked Hunter in with him so I could not get to him. Hunter was screaming and crying for me.

More occurred in between those dates, but those are some highlights, and enough to know I needed to make a permanent exodus, and quickly, for the sake of the children's and my physical, mental, and emotional health.

I found a house to buy and began packing my belongings to move out of the marital home. True to scared and vindictive form, Chester rummaged through the packed boxes and took things he did not want me to have. I knew this because I found them in various 'hiding' places around the house. Items were in places he thought I would not look or could not reach because my physical condition limited my access. He unearthed my favorite ceramic pitcher from the Metropolitan Museum of Art. The vase was inspired by Van Gogh and featured a relief of a sunflower—my favorite flower. He found it packed with some dishes and uncovered it from the protective bubble wrap, then set it on a high bookshelf. I saw it when going through the den to find anything I had overlooked. I managed to stretch and configure my body to retrieve it, thus foiling Chester's desire to deprive me of something beautiful.

In leaving the marriage to establish a home and new life, I was mindful of the need for Hunter and Garland to be around their father, and sought visitation and custody advice from an attorney. Court orders were necessary to keep Chester responsible for paying the state-mandated portion of the children's expenses and for him to visit them regularly. The visitation guidelines were basically ignored when Chester moved out of state about a month after I closed on our new residence and Hunter, Garland, and I moved in. The children were greatly affected when Chester moved away. They really missed their father, especially Hunter. Hunter prayed that his father would return to town with his fiancée to work and live—Chester met and proposed to another woman two months after leaving town. I felt responsible for Hunter's sadness, but firmly knew I had done what was best. Before the separation, Hunter had begun to stutter and was angry and anxious all of the time, and Garland had relatively shut down, not wanting to talk to anyone. When he did speak, he was quiet and vague. I could not predict these outcomes of my choice to leave Chester, but I knew I had to leave to build normalcy in life.

Friends and family immediately saw improvement in Hunter and Garland after Chester left town. Once Hunter and Garland got use to Chester being gone, their demeanor was lighter and happier, and they laughed again and were more playful. When shopping in the local home improvement store with Hunter and Garland, I ran into their godmother. With assured confidence she said, "So, Chester left town." I had not told a soul of his departure and was surprised to hear her remark. I nodded. "I could tell immediately," she added. "I see it in the children's renewed spirits." Wow, was all I thought, and 'double wow' was what I felt when Hunter's fourth-grade teacher reported that he was like a new person, more focused and determined to excel academically and socially. And, speaking of social strides, Garland became all about his friends and suddenly loved being liked and noticed for his goodness. Bingo! I had hit the jackpot and scored big for my children by following my heart in search of a better life.

My friends, one in particular, Martha from California, stood by my side the entire time the drama with Chester played out. We emailed each other regularly. Though she lived on the other side of the country, I felt every bit of the encouragement she gave as if she lived right next door. Her support, like that expressed in this email reply, helped me through…

"Your horns are showing." What a great remark you made! Yeah, I know what he was into......................jealousy, envy, anger, and a need to reduce you.......................I am so glad you are out of that life now so you have a chance to have a normal life! HOORRAY, you did the right thing to get out and STAY OUT!!!!!!!!!!!!! – M

I first met Martha about a year after the multiple sclerosis diagnosis. She became a very close friend and the person I told everything, whether it was about my family, the illness, past and present loves, or my business. You name it, she knew more about my adult life than my parents! I felt comfortable talking to her because I knew she listened, understood, gave sound advice, and was in my life to help. God brought us together, no doubt. She was part of my miracle. She was a caring and loving soul on Earth doing God's work. I am forever indebted to her and graciously testify.

Receiving My Miracle

This is my truth, as true as it is to me that I am receiving my miracle. I felt it so powerfully last night when lying in bed. It felt so good that I did not want to go to sleep. Instead, I felt the relaxation in my hips and knees and the sparks of sensations in my feet. I visualized and saw myself walking. I felt the floor underneath my feet as I took steps with my strong and flexible legs. My miracle is happening, and I repeatedly thanked God for it. I must have expressed gratitude a hundred times before going to sleep. In fact, I thanked myself to sleep and awakened the next morning with more thanks to give. That happened three days ago.

I told Martha of my experience. She is my angel who says that I am one and that I look like one, too. I remind her that my son Garland is a true angel. She agreed, and I will return to the point now... We met in a Mother's Whole Foods grocery store in Orange County over a year after the multiple sclerosis diagnosis. My marriage was on the rocks. To help save Chester and me from jumping off the cliff into irreparable splits-ville, my brother-in-law paid for my immediate family to fly to California to visit family there. It was a much-needed getaway. My husband not being gainfully employed and my dealing with symptoms I did not comprehend and could not control were taking a huge toll on the wellbeing of the family. My brother-in-law thought sending us away would help rejuvenate our spirits.

My quest for answers, relief, and a cure led me to every health food store I saw to find nutritious, chemical-free foods to nourish and strengthen my body in effort to eliminate all disease. Mother's Whole Foods, in sunny southern California, was in order. The one closest to where we were staying was well stocked with fresh organic veggies, packaged crisp Lundberg rice cakes, and a delicious made-to-order take-out delicatessen/salad bar with the option to order from a menu and dine in. I found my way to the colorful carrots and ripe radishes on display and looked through the selection. My husband and sons were in the vitamin aisle. Chester was loudly reciting the "look at what a great teacher and father I am" routine for everyone in the store to hear. Martha was browsing in the adjacent aisle and heard him. She made her way to see who was talking, and then, as she describes, was drawn to the energy radiating from my being in the produce section. She walked over to me and began talking. She noticed I was having trouble standing and asked why. I told her the brief history of the physical challenge leading to that day in Mother's:

"Over a year ago, on December 31, 1999, I went to the doctor for an annual exam and reported the fatigue I was feeling. Blood tests were ordered to see if something 'funky' was going on inside. The night after

the appointment, there was a distinct discomfort in my left side. It was most prominent in my neck and progressed through my shoulder and arm and down through my left hand. My fingers were quite numb and weak as well. The intensity subsided over days but never fully dissipated. I still have numbness and stiffness in my left hand that has leapt over to the right, and my left shoulder stiffens severely some days.

Y2K hit. In mid-January, after a winter break, it was time to return to the dance studio I own and operate to begin teaching for the new season. Ballet is my forte and my first dance love. It is not uncommon for a dancer to be exceptionally good at ballet but hate it with no reservations because it is a technique that requires perfection and exactness that can never be met. Dancing can lead to constant dissatisfaction if the expectation is to be perfect. From the 'doer' to the viewer, there is always going to be criticism that can lead to frustration. In spite of this truth, I simply love ballet. I love the way it feels to do, and I do not care what anyone thinks or says about it—that was, until I could not physically dance anymore. The euphoric feeling of dancing comes especially when taking ballet class or performing. This is probably why the love is so strong: because 99% of being a dancer is about studying and physically honing, perfecting, and demonstrating the technique. The remaining 1% is a private 'aha moment' that only the dancer knows.

'Okay, let's begin!' I enthusiastically called all dancers to collect for the beginning of the class. Everyone had a place at the barre, including me at the helm to show the first combination. 'First position, please. Port de bras, one and two,' I said; when teaching class, I simultaneously call out the combination and do it. By now, everyone was familiar with the standard warm up. When I execute combinations with the students, it reinforces what they already know while giving me a chance to work out. If anyone is new to a class on any given day, the person can simply follow along as I continued to do combinations on the right side and then on the left side at the barre.

My reason and objective for opening the studio is met with every class taught. It is the insatiable desire to dance forever. With each class taught, the dream is compounded and the objective met through relaying the steps verbally, physically, and spiritually. All I have to do is hear the music. Sometimes just hearing one or two bars is sufficient to formulate a combination. The vision of the movement is internally seen and felt when the beat and rhythm are heard. My mind knows what to do with the music and instantly tells my body how it should move."

It was not possible for me to physically demonstrate these ideas to Martha, so the next best thing for me to do was to colorfully explain the occurrence. The inflection of my voice would guide her to understand better how my once impeccably graceful and controlled body was now slowed and compromised with stiffness and weakness. How in the world this had happened seemingly overnight was beyond comprehension. One friend suggested "someone put something" on me. I know nothing about voodoo or roots and the mystics behind it, but I do believe in God and that each of us is placed on Earth for the purpose of doing His work. So here I am, a beautiful, once extremely fluid-moving ballet dancer living a very public life in which all those who see and know me know I am living a drastically altered, physically debilitated existence. It could be devastating to live with, but I do not choose to let it get me down. How many people are able to learn to walk again and feel a miracle and do it so graciously? I believe that is my charge in life. I believe what I am experiencing physically is what I agreed to take on in the spiritual realm before I was born.

I am an angel doing God's work so that the world may witness a miracle, and God brought Martha into my life so we can work together to generate the miracle. We have known each other for fourteen years. She has seen me through many life changes. The emotions accompanying the changes ranged from numbness to exhilaration to shock. I got through those life-perplexing experiences, and I am getting through this one, as well.

Three days before writing this testimony, I'd had a stretching session with a medical school graduate friend who helps me stretch my joints, including ankles, knees, hips, and left shoulder. I had not worked with him during the previous five weeks due to an intense work schedule. During that five-week period of time, I was feeling much frustration with my physical state and overwhelmed with my work responsibilities. It was production season for The Center of Dance annual performance. I shared how I was feeling with Martha. Her lighthearted response was something like, "So, you just feel fed up."

All I could do was laugh and say, "Exactly," because that was an accurate description. She laughed too. And suddenly I just did not feel as overwhelmed. She proceeded to tell me not to focus on the negative, but to keep thinking of my miracle and thanking God for it. After being stretched that night, my mother massaged my legs—she was visiting. I went to bed shortly thereafter. While lying in bed before going to sleep, I did my ritual auto-suggestion mantra as outlined by Napoleon Hill in Think and Grow Rich. *Hill says that anything you want in life can and will be achieved by following simple basic steps of writing specifically what you want in life, identifying a date for achieving the desire, and stating a plan for its achievement. The plan must be immediately acted upon once devised, and the written statement is to be read before retiring at night and upon awakening in the morning until it has been memorized and becomes a burning obsession. From there, the subconscious mind will lead to how to achieve the goal.*

My obsession with walking normally has me committed to following the protocol outlined by Napoleon Hill, as well as the one by Martha. With her, I began eliminating allergies to align my body to productively accept all vitamins, nutrients, and minerals for optimal function. The latest allergy eliminations have been Vitamin A, hormones, salt, and Vitamin D. Of particular importance is that I took her advice to pray for my miracle. I had a nose bleed and release of clotted blood from my sinuses after the Vitamin A clearing, which was amazing and wonderful, along with the exhilarating realization of my miracle of walking when lying in bed three nights ago. The euphoric feeling of receiving my miracle remains, as does the strength and flexibility in my legs.

With Martha and the rest of my support network and cheerleaders in place, I was unknowingly being positioned to add to the pot of my golden decision to strike out on my own, and the grand prize of them all would come just a short time later.

ACT 2

Moving the Bus

downstairs for concern of falling. I managed my health condition and persevered with little complaint as the independence was welcomed and I was overjoyed with being free to define the terms of our life.

I still drove and enjoyed ordinary daily activities, such as making runs to the grocery store, going to the gas station, and venturing anywhere I needed and wanted to go. The increased time it took to do anything or go anywhere was frustrating, though. It became more necessary for me to use assistive devices to function. I began to organize my time coordinating access to canes, walkers, and wheelchairs for mobility once I got out the car. Getting from the car to a building or event became more difficult to do on my own, so, I would schedule to meet with people to help me transition. My mind chattered constantly: How would I feel once I arrived at a destination and parked the car? Would I be able to get out and walk to where I needed to be? Would people be watching and would someone come to help? Such talk went on in my head each and every time I went out in public. To avoid people I knew seeing me struggle, I began going to the grocery store on the other side of town. There was no hiding when it came to going to the studio, though. First, I had to find available parking on the street outside the studio. Once parked, I had to walk to the building, and when inside climb twenty-one steps to get to the studio to teach class. I cut the time close to when I needed to be there one particular night and felt overwhelmingly rushed. I arrived at the peak traffic hour, which added to the stress. Fortunately, I found a parking space directly across the street from the building entrance. I parked, got out of the car, and leaned against it to collect my strength and confidence. I waited for an opportune time when traffic was slow, then crossed the street using one cane. It was a very hot day, and my body was extra stiff and numb from the heat and anxiety of rushing. The feeling in my legs was evaporating rapidly and, midway across the street, I stepped and collapsed. A friend came running from one of the vehicles four cars back, and a father who saw what happened while escorting his daughter to the studio came running from the sidewalk. Both of them helped me get to my feet and across the rest of the road. With their assistance, I successfully dragged myself into the building, climbed up the twenty-one stairs, and went into the studio. I felt embarrassed that my student had seen me that way. Here I was, her ballet teacher, giving lessons on poise and grace, and I could not even feel my legs to walk on my own in a coordinated fashion. I did not ask often, but I wanted to know why this was happening to me. How could a once very able-bodied dancer no longer feel her muscles, bend her knees, and lift her legs? It was a fair question, yet there was no concrete answer in my mind to the cruel irony. It was unjustifiable and just did not make sense. With no explanation from 'a place of all-knowing,' I went on to teach class and tried to stop thinking about the traffic-stopping incident.

More often, people began assisting me from my car to the studio and vise-versa. Just about every Thursday, Jane, the mother of one of my students, arrived at the same time to meet and help me before her daughter's class. She was very dedicated to her children and involved in all aspects of their activities, so I understood her deliberate concern with assisting me. She would meet me on Thursdays to help me out of the car, help me into the building, support me up the stairs, and step with me into the studio. At one of her daughter's ballet classes, she asked if she could film it to capture some childhood memories. That was fine by me, and I did not think any more about it. About three months later, Jane and another friend, Robin, approached me and told me why the footage was taken earlier. Jane had solicited other dance parents and members of the community to write letters in support of me winning a *Your Wildest Dream* prize, offered by national talk show host Oprah Winfrey. The letters got no response, however. Robin, one of the community members who supported Jane's initial efforts, was an avid fan of the weekly series *Extreme Makeover: Home Edition*, through which worthy people in need received new homes, remodeled businesses, and brand-new vehicles. Jane and Robin visited me, told me what Jane had done and suggested I apply to *Extreme Makeover: Home Edition*. "I don't know about that," was my initial response after hemming and hawing at their suggestion. I was very hesitant to do it, not wanting the public attention on such a broad scale.

"Get over it!" Robin insisted. "You need help, and these people can help you." She was right. I did need help. I thought about it some more and reasoned there was nothing to lose by applying, and so much to gain, if I was selected. And, from that moment on, I completely let the private me go. There was no more room for my ego to control things and to be on guard. To complete the application, I had to disclose my entire adult personal history, from names of past boyfriends to the number of marriages I'd had. I also had to disclose my entire adult financial history including bank and investment accounts information and if I had ever filed for bankruptcy.

The most important question asked on the application was why I felt I deserved an extreme makeover. My answer was simple—"I am a dancer who teaches dance, and I am disabled. The diagnosis is multiple sclerosis, and the disability has made it increasingly difficult to function in my home and go to my place of business to work." Writing this confession completely changed my outlook. It was freeing to reveal to others and admit to myself on paper that I needed help. My life was exposed as approved by me, and it was surprisingly okay. I willingly and freely shared aspects of my life on paper applications, in video footage, and through legal documents. Six weeks after submitting the application, I received a call from the show's casting director telling me I was one of seven applicants in my area being considered for the makeover. She said that more information was needed to decide and asked some lighter, more personal questions; she wanted to know my favorite motif (I told her it was the sun), color (orange), and flower (the sunflower).

I was not very familiar with the television show, so I began watching it regularly to get an idea of what I might be getting into. Each week a family in need was awarded a makeover for some reason, whether it was due to financial hardship after the breadwinner's death, or helping a family with a member at war, or saving conjoined twins from a mold-infested living environment. Upon seeing case after case, week after week, it became clear that my story was a fitting one to tell and the viewers would agree with me receiving a makeover. I told no one I had applied—I thought only Jane and Robin knew—so when show producers began calling more frequently, asking for more information and swearing me to secrecy as required in the application process, I had no one to talk to about what was happening or to ask for advice if I felt I needed it. Of course, my sons Hunter and Garland knew, but I forbade them from telling their father. Chester would want to know details of the application and the specifics of any agreement I signed as it pertained to the children, to see how they would benefit and what could be in it for him as a joint-custody parent. I did not put it past him to hire a lawyer and subpoena me to court for review of the application and any pertinent contractual agreements. Worse, he might contact the show production company and start demanding information. The producers would lose interest in my case and disregard my application to avoid a lawsuit and public controversy. I knew Chester well enough to be certain my concerns and fears were not far-fetched. Getting in the way of me and the children receiving the makeover would be his vindictive way of getting me back for leaving him. No, sirree. He could not know.

When the production company received everything needed to complete the application, they contacted me with news that the contest was narrowed down to three finalist families being considered in my area, and mine was one of them. They gave me a date in two weeks, when the star design team featuring Ty Pennington might come knocking at my door. The night before the designated day, I finally called my parents and told them what was going on. The dialog went something like this: "Oh, that's nice, Carol. I heard of that show before. They do really good work for good people in need." That was my mother's response. I could tell by her tone that she was being kind, but had doubts.

Daddy outright did not expect anything to come of it. "Ahhh, that show is fixed. They create these stories and sensationalize them to pull at the heartstrings of viewers to get them to watch every week and jack up ratings." There was no mistaking that my father was skeptical and did not believe.

"I don't know, Daddy, this seems real and they sound pretty legitimate to me" was my retort, and I left it at that. We went on to talk about other things, like how Hunter and Garland were doing in school and how I was getting along. When the conversation ended, I went to pack as instructed by the producer, in case there were special visitors at my door the next day and we were sent away on "vacation." My enthusiasm was somewhat deflated after talking with my folks, yet sparks of excitement flickered as I packed a week's worth of clothes, shoes, and toiletries for me, Hunter, and Garland.

From Door Knock to Dream House

We awakened extra early the morning of Sunday, December 7, 2005 to shower, dress, and be ready for the seven o'clock *Extreme Makeover: Home Edition* "Door Knock" possibility. After a hearty pancake, turkey bacon, and eggs breakfast washed down with orange juice, we went to a back room where I kept the computer, a drafting table, and a stationary elliptical walking machine. Hunter sat at the computer and plugged in his earphones to listen to music. Garland went to work on his series of super hero drawings at the drafting table, and I got a book from the book case, opened it to a marked page, and began reading. No more than fifteen minutes had passed, after we were settled when I heard a lot of commotion out front followed by a loud call to us on a megaphone.

"Carol, Hunter, Garland, wake up and come on out!" Hunter did not hear at first, but he pulled the ear plugs out of his ears and stood up when he saw Garland drop his pens and run out of the room. I knew exactly what was going on, but needed a moment to collect my two canes, stand up, find my balance, and walk to the front door.

"Woo hoo!" Hunter passed Garland and went outside first, pumping his fists up in the air in excitement. Garland followed his big brother's lead, ran out the door, and threw his arms up too.

When I finally made it to the front door, I attempted to open it. Ty ran up the stairs, opened the door fully, and helped me out. I screamed with elegant excitement and a hint of a cry in my voice, "I just want to hold you!" and reached for Ty with one arm as I held both canes for support in my other hand.

"Let me help you, sweetheart." He grabbed and hugged me.

The events that occurred afterwards that day are a blur. It was surreal, but it really happened. I was grounded enough to recall seeing the town's chief of police across the street, in my neighbor's front yard, watching the "Door Knock" aftermath action and me shouting to him, "Hey Chief Brown!" That simple acknowledgement meant a great deal to him. I know because he told me many times over the years, whenever we ran into each other. The miracle of being selected for an extreme makeover was a dream come true. As a young child and into my early adulthood, I would doodle and draw for hours the kind of house I wished to live in one day. It had big rooms to move through gracefully and an open kitchen and floor plan convenient for family and friends to congregate and socialize. The store of the universe was finally delivering to me my order of a dream house for the price of time, patience, imagination, persistence, and faith.

Carol Crawford Smith, Hunter Smith and Garland Smith with Ty Pennington, December 2005

The order became reality fast and gave me much more than what I had originally bargained for. After filming the "Door Knock," Ty and producers took Hunter, Garland, and me on a ride through Blacksburg in an oversized stretched limousine.

People walking on the sidewalks waved as we passed, and cars in motion honked on both sides of the street. Everyone in town knew who we were and what was going on. I found out over weeks, months, and years afterwards that network producers had visited town about a month prior to the day we learned we were recipients. They met with town officials, university administrators, building contractors, and others to get permits and finalize plans for the makeover build. They even spoke with my medical practitioners, my students, and anyone else who knew me, could verify I was legit, and could substantiate my story for the show script already being written. While I was made by the show producers to keep my actions secret, they were disclosing the possibility all of the time.

The reason for the ride was to take us downtown to The Center of Dance. It was Ty's "Secret Project" to renovate—a regular feature on each episode—and he wanted to see it. We pulled up to the curb after the ten minute drive from home to the studio. The children jumped out, and my friend Ann called to me as I was about to get out. She 'happened' to be downtown and ran across the street to greet me. Then, Chester's brother, who lived in an apartment above the restaurant across the street from the studio, showed up out of nowhere. I was happy to see them both, but the show producers were not pleased. They asked them to step away so they could redo the footage of Ty escorting me out of the limousine. From there we went inside the building. The cameraman filmed Ty, Hunter, Garland, and me walking into the building and stopping at the foot of the staircase. "So, here is the problem." Ty commented as he looked up at the twenty-one steps.

"Yes," I said, then began the climb, holding the banister with my right hand and both canes in my left while being assisted by Ty on that side. Hunter and Garland walked up ahead of us. The camera continued to record. "I have to take one step at a time," I stated short of breath, as I slowly lifted one leg, then the other to mount the steep staircase. There was a landing midway up, and I stopped to take a break, still being held by Ty and tightly holding the banister. My legs were wobbly and tired, but I was determined to go to the top as I had done each and every time I had to go teach.

It took twelve minutes and three stop breaks, but we finally made it up with the camera rolling throughout it all. I was neither acting nor pretending, but was consciously aware they were getting excellent footage for the show. The performer in me instinctively knew how to present genuinely and truly, with grace, dignity, and beauty, so viewers would be moved to watch more. My unintentional acts delivered abundantly. Ratings reported our two-hour episode had twenty-three million viewers when it first aired eight weeks later, on February 12, 2006. The two-hour show came in second to the opening ceremonies of the Winter Olympics, which aired the same night and time and was watched by thirty million viewers.

A well-known personality also diagnosed with multiple sclerosis came to town during the build to appear on my "Smith Family" episode and present Ty with a special monetary gift for me. The producers had revealed other footage to us when we were on 'vacation' that was not included in the final airing; thus, the footage was not seen by the viewers to verify. Still, I followed up years later to inquire and express my gratitude.

May 23, 2011

Dear Montel Williams,

I hope this note finds you in great spirits and doing extremely well. It is hard to believe that over 5 years have passed since my children and I received an extreme makeover of a new home and remodeled dance studio. Please allow me this time to update you on what is happening with us.

My son Hunter is about to graduate from high school on June 5th. He has done extremely well in his high school career both academically and in sports. He played tennis and represented his school in diving. In the latter sport, Hunter placed first in district and regional competitions and second in the Virginia High School League state diving championship competition for both years 2010 and 2011. He also achieved great honors academically and will attend University of Virginia in the fall. Waahoo, Hunter!

My younger son Garland is a sophomore in high school. School is going great for him, as well. His sport is soccer. He was the youngest to play varsity as a freshman last year and helped to bring his team to first place in the 2010 Virginia High School League state soccer championship game.

I am well and happily operating my studio for 16 years now. Your contribution during the makeover was an extreme help, as the money you presented allowed me to stay in business. In August of 2008, I moved to a new location due to a leaky roof and an unsafe environment. Though stressful at the time of emergency moving—I received notice to vacate immediately on a Wednesday, and with help from twelve community members, stripped the old studio of the makeover gift and moved into a new space over the weekend to be back in operation the following Monday—I am now operating comfortably in a new space that is accommodating and very accessible with an elevator and ample public parking, allowing me to get to the studio accessibly, as I now use a wheelchair regularly.

On March 28th, I presented Dance Theatre of Harlem Ensemble here in Blacksburg in appreciation to the community for their help with our December 2005 extreme makeover and studio mini-makeover three years later. The network producers reported that over 4000 people helped with our extreme makeover. I am forever grateful for the help, and the best way I thought to publicly express my gratitude was with a gift of dance to the community by way of the DTHE performance.

With five years having passed, in addition to updating you, I write to inquire about a statement you made upon presenting Ty Pennington with the check for me to keep my studio in operation. When on 'vacation' during the makeover the producers showed Hunter, Garland, and me the clip of you stating to Ty that you would personally continue providing an equivalent gift every five years for as long as I operate my studio. I humbly write to know if the money you promised will be granted, as it is greatly needed at this time for operations. With the studio move, rent has increased significantly, and the gift would help tremendously.

Thank you again, for everything you did to make our extreme makeover possible. And, thank you for your time to read this letter on our updates. I truly hope to hear from you soon.

Wishing you well, always,

Carol Crawford Smith

My inquiry to Montel Williams was genuine as presented to me and understood. It was worth a shot to follow up and ask—I only hoped that he would receive my letter and would one day respond. In addition to Williams' gift, we were given a beautiful one-level accessible home and remodeled dance studio. The latter of which included a lift built into the banister so I could get upstairs. I no longer had to climb steps to get to work and had full stamina and breath when it was time to teach. As for my residence, the walk throughout my house was on one level, and the low, computerized stovetop and other amenities in the kitchen were very accommodating. There were laundry facilities for both me and the children in our respective bathroom areas on opposite sides of the house. Yes, we had two wash machines, two dryers, and two full private bathrooms. There was a guest half-bathroom, too. The designers chose to include numerous aesthetically pleasing sights everywhere. Wall colors were warm earth and pastel tones of brown, green, blue, and beige in the open common areas of the entrance foyer, kitchen, dining area, and living room. There was a long hallway to the bedrooms that looked like a gallery, with colorful dishware displayed in glass cabinets and on racks. The hall walls exhibited vintage art reproductions with positive, thought-provoking imagery, and there were cast-iron bars mounted on one entire wall of the hall to help support me when walking. These functional bars were whimsical-looking and curvy and reminded me of something in a Dr. Seuss children's book. Overall, the house was a pleasure to be in and look at, both inside and out.

It felt so right living in our new home and functioning in both the first and second remodeled studios. I often reminisced about the makeover extravaganza to remind me that miracles do happen and to testify I am a witness. I think back to the day the house was revealed to us. We started the morning in a hotel room in my hometown, ordered room service, and got dressed after showering. The prior six days were spent doing similar things—we were in La Jolla, California for "vacation" while our old house was demolished and the new one was being built. We stayed in a resort there and were treated like royalty. Meals were healthy, colorful, and delicious. I was given spa treatments and spending money for entertainment. We went to the zoo. It was glamorous fun and a lifestyle that felt completely right for me, Hunter, and Garland. I knew I could definitely get used to receiving such luxuries regularly. Back in the hotel in my hometown on the morning of the house 'reveal,' to carry on with the special treatment and to spend the remaining money given to us, I made arrangements for my hair dresser to curl my hair and trim the boys'. We had to look good. There would be cameras recording our reaction to seeing the house for the first time. This was the climax of the show and the main reason people watched. There would be people watching who I knew from past and present, as well as those I did not know at all. It could be a chance to be seen by a director and asked to do a role in a Hollywood movie or on a television show. The possibilities in my imagination were endless.

After the show aired, I did go on the Montel Williams Show; it was "The Faces of MS" episode. I did not receive any other film or TV offers, but I was finally living in my dream house. It was exactly what I wanted and what I would have created if I had sat down with the designers and architects and described it. They precisely conceived the perfect home for me based on my responses to application questions like, 'What would you hate to see in your new house?' and 'What color would you not like to see in your bathroom?'

My best answers were "I'd hate to see my new house without hardwood floors, and the color pink would not be appreciated in my bathroom like my favorite color orange would." The orange and beige tiled walls of the bathroom that I used every day, and the beautifully finished hardwood floors I travelled throughout my house prove that my desired outcomes were understood. There were no flower boxes—a feature once upon a time desired for my picture-perfect house—instead, there were raised stone flower beds out front with Japanese maple trees that beautifully altered year round, reflecting each season, complimented by purple and yellow pansies. The house was more than a dream, it was a perfect miracle made possible by none other than God. How else would more than 4000 people from the community and beyond galvanize to make the dream of a home and improved accessible business come true, if not by divine ordinance? People who did not know me, but had heard my story drove for miles around the region, as well as from out of state, to help. An abundance of heartwarming stories were shared of how people came together in love and care to help my children and me. To me, this suggested that we were placed in a position for good work in humanity to occur and be witnessed by millions.

There were so many people to thank. Though I did not know them all, I expressed public gratitude to whomever I could whenever I could. I placed a full-page thank-you letter in the paper, and I expressed my appreciation during the community viewing after the episode first aired...

> *"I sit here, in extreme appreciation, watching our makeover show, and think about all of the people who have endlessly and unselfishly helped me since I set foot in this town and branched out to be of service to the community. The list is endless. There are two individuals I wish to acknowledge right here and now. They are Jane Weiseman and Robin Price Grubbs, along with their husbands and, also, their children, who are growing up with my sons, Hunter and Garland. It took Jane and Robin and a community of loving supporters, including major contributors Building Specialists,*

Newcomb Electric, and Virginia Tech, to build our house and remodel The Center of Dance, so we could continue to reside in Blacksburg and serve the community through the business. I moved here from New York City fourteen years ago, single with seven suitcases and two cats. I did not know a soul. Yet over the years since, I have seen some of you born, and I have seen you play your first soccer game. You, in turn, have seen me over the years in full dance form and strength suddenly having to function through a debilitating illness while dealing with the challenges and triumphs of marriage and becoming a single mother. You have been my pillars of strength, and some of you I can call upon when I need to let my guard down or receive a helping hand. You know us well and understand the development and makings of our household. If ever needing a support network, I know you are there. Thank you for this assurance, and for your love, care, and tremendous makeover gift."

Building Specialists, Inc. Ad, December 2005

After the show aired, a multitude of letters, emails, and phone calls came to me. I received correspondence from people I knew and did not know from my town and from all over the nation, including incarcerated prisoners in public penitentiaries. When the show later aired in syndication, I received more heartfelt communication from people in the United States and abroad, expressing gratitude and care. I happily received fan mail at my studio website, too—*Messages are unedited. Names and email addresses have been changed:*

Name: Maribeth Walker
Email: wlkmar@aol.com

I watched extreme makeover tonight and I was so touched by Carol's story and more moved by her spirit. Just wanted to stay God bless her and WoW!!

Name: Pat Harrison
Email: Patharrison@comcast.net

Hi Carol, you are truly an inspiration to ALL. I saw your story on television and it brought tears of joy, pride and praise for you. One of my best friends has MS. How do I help her without being too overbearing? How do I be there for her? How can I best be a friend? As a person who works in the disabled community, I must say you are a light in the midst of a dark cloud.

Name: Bri
Email: glow@textfree.us

You taught me to never give up even if you are not doing so well and if you can't continue to don't get down on yourself! :) Thank you so much!

Name: R.J.
Email: richard@gmail.com

Dear Miss Smith, I just caught the episode of your extreme makeover on TV Land, a rerun from 2006. It was on in the background while I was doing homework, but your story caught my attention and I ended up watching the whole program. You are truly inspirational and a beautiful person inside and out. Your fortitude and spirit are admirable. I am in a 6 year relationship with somebody who was a dancer, as well, when he developed scoliosis, and your story of perseverance and overcoming inspired him to realize he is still a dancer, too. I'm not sure if you realize it, but your story is changing people's lives for the better. That is the greatest gift a person can give another. Thank you so much for having the courage to go on television because you touched two people today, 6 years after your episode even aired. May God bless you and your beautiful family, and thank you, again. Best wishes and regards, R.J.

I was so honored to receive the numerous emails and all the other contacts, and amazed by how many people were touched and inspired by my story and the show. Believe it or not, I felt blessed—in a way—to be diagnosed with multiple sclerosis and to be placed in a position to inspire humanity and to receive a dream home and an opportunity to further build my business in the process. Second to having Hunter and Garland, the extreme makeover extravaganza was the greatest miracle to happen in my life at that point, and I know it could have never happened without so many generous souls being divinely led.

While it was all occurring, however, I was wishing there were a magic wand to wave that would relieve the multiple sclerosis symptoms I was enduring, or a big bag of tricks to pull out a cure for the devastating and debilitating disease. There was no such miracle or luck, however. Maybe this is because I had not drawn any pictures of the multiple sclerosis symptoms' dissipation or kept the demise of multiple sclerosis in my mind long enough. Sadly, it persisted, but I did too, in full faith that my imagination would devise a healed body for me to live, laugh, and love in for the rest of my days.

I am so sure of my healing and full recovery to walking and dancing. Being grateful to God for the healing and calling on others to help expedite the miracle have supported my faith. I am so sure of this belief that (in my dreams) I reached out to two talk-show hosts, one of who, Oprah Winfrey, provided *Your Wildest Dreams*—the other of who is one of the funniest and most positive personalities I have seen on TV; Ellen Degeneres. I contacted them to offer an exclusive opportunity to bring my physical victory to the attention of the world. Call me crazy and delusional, if you will, but my premise is always to Ask, Believe, and Receive. One of the celebrities should surely see the inspirational message my story brings...

Dear Oprah Winfrey (Ellen Degeneres),

I send this letter with an abundance of love and passion in my being. Heck, I am love and passion. I love life, and I love people. I have a passion for dance and for sharing the healing and life-changing energy of dance with others.

In 1994, I founded a dance studio to dedicate my life to nurturing all clients' as well as an entire community's enthusiasm for dance. On February 2, 2000, I was diagnosed with a debilitating disease, multiple sclerosis. Since the diagnosis, I went from dancing gracefully to limping, to walking with a cane, then a walker, and now I use a wheelchair or electronic chair most of the time. There are days when I wake up or go to bed that I cannot feel my extremities, mainly my legs. (In fact, my hands are going numb as I type this letter.) Needless to say, I have been without the ability to dance since soon after the diagnosis.

Thankfully, throughout the ordeal, my business remains intact. In fact, it was recently featured and renovated by the crew of Extreme Makeover: Home Edition. I now have many talented and qualified instructors who teach at the studio and help keep the dream alive. The business is surviving, and the community continues to benefit from the excellence in dance provided.

The gift of a makeover is tremendous and for it, I am extremely grateful. Yet while the producers of Lock and Key Productions were the catalyst to galvanize more than 4000 people to actualize the makeover, I still remain without the ability to dance. To be able to dance is what I truly desire. And I know within me the desire exists and is stronger now than ever before.

I write to you because I believe you have the ability to effect miraculous change. I too know I have this ability within, and I believe I have been presented with this challenge to become a better person while going through it and to get over it and inspire millions more in the process. It is my desire to dance again, and it is my gift to those who will accept it to share the course of my journey from being wheelchair bound to being up and on my feet dancing. I am asking you to help me realize this dream. I am asking you to help position my life and document my story of recovery.

As a single mother of two boys, I am raising my sons to be outstanding young men. I tell them daily that all things are possible and that they can achieve whatever they choose and to always feel free to ask others to help them realize their goals and dreams. Well, I live to be a shining example to my sons and ask that you help me to realize the goal to recover from a debilitated state, and dance again for the world to see.

Thank you for the time to read my letter and consider my request. I admire and I am inspired by what you do daily to enter the lives of others with stories of hope, happiness, and love. I send you best wishes for eternal success and abundance.

Always,

Carol Crawford Smith

P.S. Enclosed please find a DVD of the Extreme Makeover: Home Edition episode featuring the story of my family's house and business makeover. Enjoy!

Until these women respond, I tell and share my story with the world myself. So, here I am sharing many details about me from my very private, personal side once known by only a few, if any, and moving those details to the open, public side known by masses. I was hesitant to expose either side, or anything in between, for fear of people seeing me and my life in a way contrary to how I think I am perceived. Thinking that way boils down to me living a lie, though, and if there is one thing I have learned in my half-life of living, it's that I must be honest no matter how much I think it will hurt me or someone else, especially when no harm is intended in me being open and sincere.

ACT 3

We Are Family

SCENE 5

One

"FROM THE MOMENT I FIRST saw my baby, that delicate bundle of joy was the most beautiful and perfect human being I'd ever seen. The child was exactly who I had greatly desired and was more perfect then I had envisioned in my picture-perfect family composition. I could not have asked for a greater gift."

At the time of the extreme makeover, Hunter, Garland and I had each other, a loving community of family and friends, and a home. In a secure and stable frame of mind and existence, I saw lovingly and fearlessly to reflect and comment on our family, and the beautiful effect my children had on me, starting with my first born: My baby was due to arrive on August 18, 1993. I had swollen and ballooned up to 186 pounds by two weeks after the due date, when the OB/GYN decided to induce labor and scheduled me to go into the hospital for the induction. I knew my life would change forever once I went to the hospital, and I wanted to go there when I felt the baby was absolutely ready to be born, and I was absolutely ready to give birth. After awakening, I showered, got dressed, and had a good breakfast. Once the hospital bag was double checked and packed to my satisfaction and the obstetrician's recommendations, my maternal instincts told me it was time to go.

Chester and I walked into the hospital at about 8:30 AM. Upon checking in, I was brought a wheelchair to sit in, and Chester and I were escorted up to the maternity floor. The journey there was contemplative. I took in the atmosphere and spirit of the surroundings as the attendant rolled me past a room where a woman was lying and holding an infant. We rolled through a birthing area and into a room with an empty bed. The cold and sterile atmosphere of the space made me more aware of the seriousness and formality of giving birth in a hospital. There were steel medical tables in the white-walled rooms, and poles on wheels with monitors for IVs. It is not the setting I'd once thought I desired to give birth in, but it felt more right being there than being at home with a midwife, especially since I was fourteen days overdue without one sign of a contraction or a hint that the baby was coming.

Chester and I had no idea of the baby's sex either. We'd had an ultrasound seven months earlier, hoping to find out the sex, but the baby would not hold still for us to determine if it was male or female. The image we saw was of the little being executing back flip after back flip in the amniotic fluid. Seeing the baby move in that manner gave me a better understanding of why I had an abundance of butterfly-flurry-like sensations throughout the early months of pregnancy. When the baby grew bigger and stronger, not only could you feel it "kick" but you could actually see it rotating and moving from side to side, like when an object is stretched and rolled within latex. Then, finally, on September 1, 1993, at forty-two weeks in gestation, the day and moment was upon us for the flipping, rotating little human inside of me to be its own entity in the world.

The nurses gave me a hospital robe to put on when we got settled in the room. It was the kind of robe that completely covered the front of the body and tied at two areas at the upper back. I put the robe on with assistance and climbed into the high bed to wait for the doctor. Chester had been given a set of hospital scrubs to wear and had left to put them on. When he re-entered the room looking like a doctor, I felt proud and comforted, knowing we were in the right place and were being given the right attention in order to deliver the perfect baby. When I was settled in the bed and Chester was comfortable in a chair, my doctor appeared. "So, you finally decided to join us," she commented upon entering the room and walking to my bedside. I presumed she was alluding to my late arrival for a seven o'clock appointment, but I also knew I had to take my time and be in the right frame of mind and comfortable. Having a baby was not about business and punctuality, for me. My spirit of entitlement took a strong hold and led me to do what I felt best for me and my baby. If I had arrived "late," then so be it.

I smiled at the doctor and told her I was happy to be there and that I was ready to have my baby. She acknowledged cordially, monitored me, checked on the equipment, and left with a pleasant demeanor. Next thing I knew, several nurses were in the room preparing me and the equipment for birth. Sacks of liquid were hooked up to the IV pole, and a needle was stuck in the most prominent vein of my right hand to set up for the infusion. I abhor needles, and the thought and act of having a sharp object inserted in my body and a port remaining at the top of my hand was painful and disconcerting. The procedure was a necessary step to take, though, if labor was going to be induced. I wanted and was ready to have my baby, and turned my attention to being at peace and grateful rather than hurt and scared. Forty-two weeks of a human incubating in me was two weeks too long according to science and to the eager and bloated mother-to-be that was me.

The sacks of liquid were opened, and the one containing Pitocin began to slowly and steadily drip into the long clear plastic tube connected to the port in my hand. The chemical was infused into my body as prescribed. Time passed. I felt constant cramps but no major contractions. Dilation progressed from little to fair, but not enough to convince the medical team that I would have a natural delivery. Someone chose to call my case as such, and two male doctors—one tall, lean, and elderly with grey strands of hair swept across and to the right side of his balding head and the other shorter, younger, and round with a full head of short black hair—entered the room intending to prepare everyone and everything for a cesarean section. The figures and the notion were surreal. First of all, I recognized only one of the doctors, and neither was my regular OB/GYN. She had gone off duty by that time. Second of all, I was adamant about having a vaginal delivery. My baby was not going to be cut out of me, especially not for the convenience of time, money, and practice of someone I did not know. I told them no, and to be patient. I was more than certain that I could deliver naturally. The doctors did not object and soon left.

In little time, the cramping turned to pulling, shifting, and stretching. I felt like I imagine taffy would feel if it had nerves. A phenomenon far greater and sweeter than confection, which had been months in the making, was upon us in this world. I could feel the baby separate and divide from me. I could feel the baby lowering from my center and moving through my expanding and contracting birth canal. Maybe it hurt, maybe it did not. For some, it would have hurt, but for me it was a most beautiful and welcomed feeling. There were no descriptive words in this universe to explain what it was like. The experience was ineffable; it was inexpressible. I felt the moment and the movement happening, and I felt me inside of me, making it happen. I felt both at the same time and called the experience symbiotic non-dimensional—a term I created, inspired by the "inculcating wisdom" lessons of Chester.

My baby quickly went from being securely fastened and nestled in me to a human moving through me. The experience was numbing and comforting. When the crown of my baby's head shown, the older doctor—who had returned when the most definite yanking and maneuvering was occurring in me—chose to attach a plunger-like instrument to the crowning head to pull my baby out as I pushed. When the final measure of my baby—the tip of the toe—was released and independent of me, I heard a cry. The doctor held my baby up and said, "It's a boy."

Those words registered as precisely right. "Of course, he is a boy," I thought in absolute agreement. He could not possibly have been anyone other than who he was.

From the moment I first saw my baby, that delicate bundle of joy was the most beautiful and perfect human being I'd ever seen. He had straight jet-black hair and ethereal coal-black pupils in the center of shimmering, light brown irises on pristine fields of white. The child was exactly who I had greatly desired and was more perfect then I had envisioned in my picture-perfect family composition. I could not have asked for a greater gift. He was quickly cleaned, wrapped snugly in a blanket, and placed on my chest to hold. We were asked, "What's his name?"

Chester was standing next to me by the bed, with one hand on the wrapped baby and the other holding my hand. He looked at me for assurance and said, "Hunter Nathanael." I nodded in agreement, as that was the name we had agreed upon if our baby was a boy.

We returned home two days after the birth. Hunter grew amazingly, by leaps and bounds. From infanthood to adolescence, he achieved all of the expected milestones, from walking to talking to being groomed for brilliance. Hunter was a very happy child with an incredible memory, who loved to be read to. His favorite childhood books were *Goodnight Moon*, *The Little Engine that Could*, and *Are You My Mother* by Dr. Seuss. When I read the books to him, he would recite the stories verbatim as each page turned. Hunter had an impressionistic imagination. He would lie on the bed, studying the ceiling shadows at different times of the day, and say, "I wonder how you would paint that." It was evident early on that he had the mind of a genius, one who loved to talk sensibly and contemplate frequently.

Hunter showed great athletic promise early on, too. The synchronized swimming-type repetitive spiraling he exhibited in-utero transformed into tumbling, swimming, and flipping as soon as he could control and lift his body weight. He was doing forward rolls on the couch almost as soon as he could walk his roly-poly booty around the living room. When he discovered the couch had springs that enabled him to jump high and flip, his rolls turned to front layouts, landing flat on his back. Every field, hill, or span of area to tread that he came upon when outdoors was open territory for a tumbling line of cartwheels and round offs. Hunter did tricks with fearless confidence at an early age and showed little to no adversity to accomplishing great feats on his own.

Growing Up and Becoming More Autonomous

As Hunter grew from baby to toddler to little boy, his outward happiness and highly-verbal expressiveness around me and the family he was around most regularly—my parents and his two-years-younger brother, Garland—receded, and he became less outgoing. This was more pronounced as he grew older, especially after it became apparent that Chester and I neither should nor could continue to be together. I had begun to notice changes in Hunter during elementary school, from the end of third grade into the beginning of fourth grade, and I thought it was because of the distress in the family resulting from the constant fighting between Chester and me. Hunter began stuttering when talking and would cry over the littlest things. I was so caught up in my own turmoil and need to make sound decisions that I could not decipher how he and his brother were developing and affected by the familial change, or how to most effectively address it. So, I let go of trying to "fix" things and trusted that life would work it all out for the best as I followed my heart and intuition to do what I felt right for Hunter, Garland, and me.

After Chester left town, when Hunter was in fourth grade and the boys and I moved to our permanent residence, his teacher and Godmother noticed an immediate change in his spirit and demeanor. Hunter became much lighter, happier, and more carefree. The stuttering and crying stopped. He began laughing again and became more playful. Hunter thrived in activities that he could do by himself—for instance, the acrobatic feats that he constantly executed and could not seem to get enough of. When I finally bought a trampoline—after he persisted and I let go of liability concerns—it was a major draw that brought him home happy and kept him occupied after school. He would spring and flip back layout after back layout, seemingly nonstop, starting once he got off the school bus and continuing before, after, and in-between snacks, homework, dinner, and bedtime. Hunter could flip by himself 'for days' and be perfectly content. He would also encourage his brother, and a little friend or two, to try, but he was always so much more accomplished, coordinated, and fearless.

Now I will fast forward four to eight years—during which time included the extreme makeover—to when Hunter was in high school. He had a few select friends with interests in common—though not one could flip like him. I used to think that he chose to be a recluse who had just a few close friends and was determined to focus on doing well in school. He did not have a steady girlfriend in high school, but he had very good friends who were girls. He called two of them, Amy and Jennifer, his "wives." Amy was the girl who would eventually be his senior prom date, and Jennifer, his tennis buddy, was the girl who asked him—when he was a freshman—to be her senior prom escort. Hunter would joke with them about all the babies they would have, and they would list the outlandish names they would give the babies, like Aquafina, Dansani, and Nestle—ah, I can hear Hunter giggling about that now. Another girl, Sandy, made cakes for Hunter for each of his birthdays while in high school. Yet another girl, Phyllis, would take bites of his hamburger when she visited him at our home, and they made meals together. Marsha and Hunter always did extra-curricular diving together. After remembering these girls and noting their association with Hunter, I must admit that he did have many important close friends, with all of whom he had the fun that mattered and who made a positive difference in his life.

When Hunter introduced me to his "girlfriends," I noted he was mindful to be in the company of so many smart and talented females. I had greatly hoped he would ask one of the young ladies—the one of my particular liking—to be his steady girl. I trusted Hunter's choice of friends, and I was happy to know that he had found people to open up to and he was able to let his guard down when in their company. I also wanted Hunter to know it was important and necessary for me to meet his friends. I had hoped that this knowledge would cause Hunter to be nice to me and to talk to me more, like he had when he was younger. To my distain, he had become distant and unaccommodating when he got older. It was as if he wasn't allowed to be nice to me. I figured the silent-treatment and pushing-me-away acts he had started to display were typical of a teenage boy. He only let me see his anger, resentment, and frustration when he did talk to me. It was so contrary to the delight and joy he showed when being with his girlfriends—admittedly, I was jealous. For brief moments, Hunter would make physical contact with me via the air that breezed by when he brushed past me upon returning home from school. Then he would retreat to his room to do homework and stay there for the rest of the night. He would emerge from his "cave" on schedule to eat and to leave for diving, gymnastics, or tennis practice, or to be with his girlfriends.

Hunter's relating to me improved once he was in college at the University of Virginia. The improvement may have come as a result of him feeling free to express his needs while away from home in an expanded, like-minded circle of acquaintances. When he was not in classes, or when he was not in office hours with his professors, or when he was not tutoring peer undergrads, Hunter spent his days, nights, and weekends in the library at UVA studying with other Cavalier brainiacs. I was very proud of Hunter for being recognized for his high scholastic and strong leadership abilities, which led him to be selected for a position as a paid mathematics and physics tutor at UVA. Hunter also sought venues to hone and develop his innate love for swimming, tumbling, and flipping when he was in college. He had invested much time in aquatic activities in high school as a champion diver, and as a lifeguard at the pool in Blacksburg. Once in college, he continued to lifeguard and became a member of the UVA gymnastics and silks club team, where he further mastered tumbling and acrobatic skills while flying high, within, and around silky elastic bands suspended above and amid crowds of pleased and awestruck viewers. Hunter knew happiness, freedom, and love when he followed his heart and instinct to study, learn, and perform as he was physically and intellectually born to do.

The innocent, joyful, easy, and free spirit that Hunter had been as a small child had gradually evaporated—in my point of view—during the ten years that Chester was not a constant physical presence in his life, and I was digressing physically. I wanted so desperately to be my whole physical self, swimming with Hunter, riding bikes with Hunter, and especially, dancing, with Hunter, so we could grow closer and have joy together. He reached a point where it was emotionally difficult for him to help me and, with Chester living elsewhere, he felt constantly torn between his parents. He loved both Chester and me equally, and he felt that he could not show more love and attention to either one of us. He tended to side with Chester more, though, because—to paraphrase Hunter—he'd rather deal with me being upset then his father being angry—which, I'd observed, made Hunter anxious and nervous. He knew I'd get over whatever was upsetting me, and I'd always be there for him. Hunter also felt sorry for Chester because he was alone. Being there for his father and vice versa was important to him. He felt it would hurt his father if Chester felt that he was there more for me than for him. If that happened, then his father would stop being there for him, and Chester being there for him is what Hunter had prayed for and wanted so desperately once Chester and I separated. It was all so confusing. Hunter once told me, "It was so unfair for a child to have to choose." The pain of disappointment in Hunter's voice, which reflected his torn heart, had me longing for words and actions that I could use to mend what was broken and hurting in him, in me, and in our family. I had always hoped that Hunter would come out from behind the invisible wall that he had built between us causing his silence and minimal expression toward me, and in that moment, expressing the unfairness he felt of having to choose between parents, he did.

Hunter and I had once been so close and had great fun together. I was his ballet teacher from age three to twelve. For nine years in the dance studio, I helped and watched him grow and develop into a confident artistic phenomenon. From the studio to the stage to the world, he executed exceptional technique, poise, grace, and rhythm with humble humility and endearing sensitivity. There wasn't a step he would not try and leave with finished accomplishment, or a person, from dance mate to school classmate to authority figure, who he would not hesitate to help, uplift, and respect, if he could, on the way to achieving his own personal best.

I wanted Hunter to remain open and transparent to sharing and exhibiting his remarkable ways with me. Call me selfish, call me greedy, but I wanted the miracle of Hunter, for me, to see and receive, forever. Everyone who knew him wanted the same. He was not meant to be exclusively mine, though. He was here to reinforce hope in humanity, and to the entire human race he was drawn to give his whole self and to love unconditionally.

Surreal News

On Wednesday, December 17, 2014, I awakened as usual at 7:00 AM and remained in bed, waiting for my helper to arrive and assist me in my morning routine in preparation for an eleven o'clock dentist appointment. I had gotten dressed, combed my hair, and brushed my teeth by 10:20 AM and watched for the Blacksburg Transit Access bus, due to pick me up at 10:30 AM. I arrived at my dental appointment in plenty to time to speak with the appointment and financial coordinators at the front desk. I gave each coordinator updates on Hunter and Garland—former patients of the practice—and went back to the examination room to have my teeth cleaned. After being picked at, flossed, rinsed, and sucked at by a saliva ejector for a good twenty minutes, the dentist was called in for a final check. Satisfied and pleased, she dismissed me with instructions to come back in six months. My bus was scheduled to pick me up from the dentist in an hour, so I went to the nearby grocery store to get food and flowers for my household and holiday gifts for my helpers.

The bus arrived. With the help of the driver, me and the grocery items I had purchased were loaded on board. There was a mother and daughter on the bus as well, so we had a "ride-along." The conversation was fun and joyful for the entire three-minute ride home. We talked and laughed about family gatherings during the holidays and all the drama that can come with it. Once home and off the bus, the driver escorted me to my front door, and we exchanged pleasant goodbyes. When I walked into the house, I saw Garland engaged as he had been before I left for the appointment. He was home from college on winter break, sitting in the living room working on a laptop computer. He approached me soon after I entered the house. "The police came by after you left. Here's his card. He wants you to call him." Garland handed me a business card from one of the officers who visited.

"Did he say what he wanted?" I asked.

Garland said, "No, but he told me, 'Don't worry. You're not in trouble.'" I called the officer, and he was not in. I called two more times and reached him. He asked if I was home, and I told him yes. He said that he'd be right over. I had no idea why the police had come to the house. My thoughts shifted to calling Hunter, and then I thought that maybe they had stopped by to present a "Secret Santa" gift. I had recently watched a video where a very wealthy man gave a police department somewhere out West $100,000.00 cash with instructions to give $1,000.00 to 100 people in need. Maybe I was about to receive such a blessing. Inwardly excited about the possibility, I asked Garland again if he had any idea what they wanted. He told me no.

The doorbell finally rang. I asked who it was. The officer stated his name, and I opened the door. Two uniformed officers and a plainclothes man entered. I smiled and welcomed them. The lead officer introduced himself, the other officer, and the man in plain clothes, who was a chaplain.

Garland was sitting at the far end of the table. I sat in my wheelchair in the entrance foyer, facing the three men. Their demeanor did not suggest they were about to present a surprise. With definite purpose, the leading officer said, "There is no other way to say this. Hunter is deceased."

His report ripped through me like a silent stealth bullet, with no pain on impact or throughout the deepening penetration. In the micro-fraction of the second between his words and my reaction, my energy warped and personified into distorted beings rippling, waving, and rolling in slow motion to the rhythm of my abrupt outcry. "Oh God no! Oh God no! Oh God no! Oh God no! Oh God no!" I repeated the plea over and over in the same strong tone, with few tears but with definitiveness. I was well aware. At some point during my response to the news, Garland made his way to my side and took my hand.

I wanted to know what happened. The reporting officer could not say because he did not know, but he gave me the name and number of an investigating officer to call. I immediately called the investigator. He was not in, so I left a message with the precinct operator and requested an immediate returned call. Way too much time passed, so I called again and again. By the third try, the investigator was in. He could not say conclusively how Hunter passed. He could tell me, however, that Hunter was found dead in his apartment in the bathroom, hanging from a shower rod with a belt around his neck. He was naked. Evidence would need to be gathered in order to draw a conclusion as to whether his death was an accident, murder, or suicide.

I said I would tell Hunter's father and gave Chester's number to the investigator, then ended the call. I immediately began to call Chester on my cell phone, but stopped when Garland advised we use his cell phone instead. He called Chester, and when Chester answered, Garland turned on the speaker phone and told him, "Mommy has something to tell you."

I spoke, telling Chester we were on the speaker phone and that two officers and a chaplain were with Garland and me. Then I delivered the news in the exact way it had been told to me. "WHAT! WHAT! WHAT! This is tragic!" Chester exclaimed.

The news of Hunter's untimely, blindsiding death did not make sense. How could it be possible? I had just spoken with him the day before. He was on a bus in Charlottesville that Tuesday, having just gotten a haircut. He sounded so happy and laughed often during our conversation. Hunter's last winter break at UVA had just begun. His final exams, papers, and projects were complete, and he was looking forward to flying to the west coast on Saturday to spend a week with family in California. He was looking forward to the trip with great enthusiasm. He had told me that, when in California, he planned to decide the next step he would take after graduation. How could he be gone? How could my loving, humble, brilliant Hunter, with so much potential for a bright future, no longer be in this world?

There were no immediate answers to be had on the day that Hunter died, but there were many immediate actions to take, and all that needed to be done occurred expediently, like breathing. Hunter's body was cremated, his obituary was posted in the paper, and his family and friends, all those who loved him, met in a packed "standing-room only" church sanctuary six days later for a celebration of his life.

Within three months, I established a memorial scholarship in Hunter's honor.

The "One" Memorial Scholarship Honoring
Hunter Nathanael Smith (BHS Class of 2011)

Established by

Carol Crawford Smith

Hunter Nathanael Smith, also known as "One" by his mother, Carol Crawford Smith, and others close to him, was a scholar and a gentleman who accomplished great academic, athletic and social achievements in his short twenty-one years of mortal life. The "One" Memorial Scholarship Honoring Hunter Nathanael Smith (BHS Class of 2011) is awarded to a senior graduating from Blacksburg High School and continuing his or her education at a four-year college. Upon graduating from high school in June of 2011, Hunter Nathanael Smith matriculated at the University of Virginia in fall of the same year. Hunter Nathanael Smith chose a Mathematics major and Environmental Science minor at UVA and received a posthumous Bachelor of Arts degree in May of 2015.

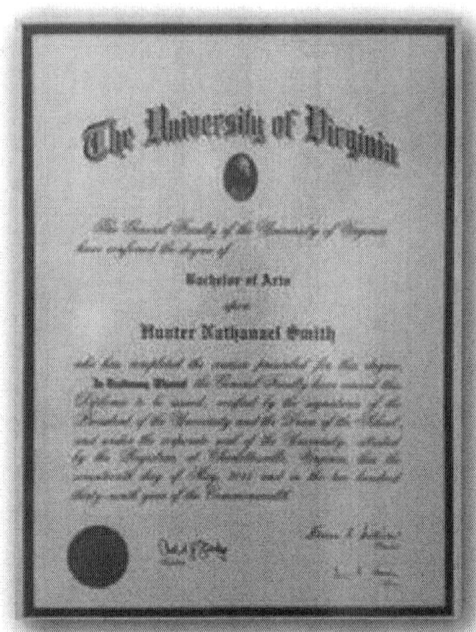

Hunter Nathanael Smith's
UVA diploma, May 2015

Hunter Nathanael Smith was proficient at learning languages and was a gifted dancer, as first taught by his mother, as well as a self-taught piano player. Hunter Nathanael Smith treasured the joys of life with his beloved family and friends, from tubing on the New River to hiking up the Cascades. Always generous with his time, he was a tutor in differential equations, statistics, and physics to his college peers, a swimming and gymnastics teacher to local children, and an avid karaoke aficionado. Hunter Nathanael Smith truly loved living and giving of his time and expertise to others with endless, unselfish caring and kindness. Above it all, Hunter Nathanael Smith had a genuine desire to do good for mankind and to save the world.

As Hunter Nathanael Smith had a love for math and science, during his college career, he was a research assistant in the photovoltaic lab and the plant pathology lab at Virginia Tech, and his love and appreciation for the subjects is immortalized at the Blacksburg Children's Museum through the Hunter Nathanael Smith Learning Laboratory, featuring the microscope bed, microscopes, and lab furniture he was awarded on Extreme Makeover: Home Edition in 2005.

Hunter Nathanael Smith had aspirations to travel overseas to work in the areas of environmental science and education. His fun-loving, kind and gentle spirit, as well as his compassion for others, led him to study many cultures and languages, including Chinese, Hindi, Hebrew, and Spanish, and to engage in their respective cultures. In familiar social environments, Hunter Nathanael Smith was known to unpretentiously break out in words and acts with his beautiful, infectious smile and happy, contagious laughter, speaking in a foreign language or doing a back flip as easily as sitting on a chair.

Hunter Nathanael Smith was a member of the swim club, acrobatics club, and gymnastics club, and was employed as both a lifeguard and math tutor at the University of Virginia. Hunter Nathanael Smith was also an employed lifeguard and swim teacher, as well as a competitive swimmer at the Blacksburg Aquatic Center. His great appreciation and respect for water sports and water safety, along with his fervent, intensely spirited, and graceful pyrotechnics enabled him to place second in the state of Virginia in years 2010 and 2011, representing Blacksburg High School in the Virginia High School League AA State Diving Championship competitions.

Hunter Nathanael Smith was a Bronze Subscribing Life NAACP Youth Member and was officially active in the organization, serving in several officer positions in the local chapter Montgomery County Youth Council. Hunter was a recipient of the Asbury United Methodist Church Scholarship for collegiate academic achievement for four years and was a member of the church's school and youth groups.

In summation, Carol Crawford Smith's "Hunter-One" or "One", as she adoringly called her son, grew from a darling, inquisitive, and precocious child raised by a single mother to become a highly intelligent, academically and athletically gifted man who was both encouraged and supported by nurturing, loving, and diverse communities of family and friends. As Hunter Nathanael Smith was a well-rounded, multi-talented, and diversely accomplished human being whose interests and associations in life epitomized inclusion, ALL Blacksburg High School students, including students affiliated with any Blacksburg High School clubs, are encouraged to apply.

Application criteria:

- *Blacksburg High School graduating senior*
- *Accepted to a four-year college*
- *Completed The "One" Memorial Scholarship Honoring Hunter Nathanael Smith (BHS Class of 2011) Application Form*
- *An 850-word essay referencing applicant's social, academic, and athletic involvements and applicant's vision for global change and helping others is required. Feel free to include academic interests and achievements in science, math, and learning languages. Well-rounded interests, aspirations, and goals in travelling internationally are suggested inclusions, as well.*

So the scholarship was inclusive; it was open to all BHS students to apply. That is how Hunter was—inclusive and accepting—and I know he would approve.

Four months after he passed, Hunter's death was officially ruled accidental. Evidence implied that it was a tragically fatal case of auto-erotic asphyxiation. Wikipedia describes auto-erotic asphyxiation as the term used when the act of erotic asphyxiation or breath-control play—the intentional restriction of oxygen to the brain for the purposes of sexual arousal—is done by a person to themselves. There is a stigma or taboo attached to the practice, making people reluctant to acknowledge auto-erotic asphyxiation as the cause of death in hundreds of cases. According to an FBI estimate, between 500 and 1,000 Americans die from auto-erotic asphyxiation every year. I did more research and found an article on the internet on *The Independent's* Health page headed, "When masturbation can be fatal: The practice of auto-erotic asphyxia is often concealed by a coroner's verdict. Monique Roffey looks at a lethal taboo." In the article, Roffey says, "Auto-erotic asphyxia is a method of increasing sexual excitement by restricting the oxygen supply to the brain, usually by tightening a noose around the neck. Although usually associated with hardcore sexual masochists it often arouses interest among the less experienced-curious schoolboys and young men keen to experiment with masturbation in the belief that the practice heightens sensation at orgasm. While rumours about how and why to do it abound in all-male locker rooms and dormitories, what is not passed on is the fact that it can be fatal." Auto-erotic asphyxiation is practiced mostly by men who seek heighten sexual pleasure. I, Carol Crawford Smith, add as a public service announcement that it should NOT be done alone, if at all!

I believe, as a risk taker who would fearlessly flip and dive with confidence and ease, Hunter would be okay with restricting oxygen to his brain for the purpose of sexual arousal, expecting to receive pleasure and remain alive, not to seek harm or pain—he would not intentionally hurt himself or anyone, as he was very happy at the end of his life and had so much joy to live for. As a young scientist, Hunter may not have been fully aware of the fatal danger associated with this activity. As MedicineNet.com reports, "When you rob your brain of oxygen (asphyxia), you experience a high—euphoria, dizziness, and lowered inhibition—before you lose consciousness." I conclude: My beautiful Hunter Nathanael Smith lost consciousness in sexual ecstasy resulting from practicing auto-erotic asphyxiation and did not reawaken.

Oh Hunter, my precious, One,

There are many random questions that I did not get to ask you that I want to know now: Like, in your search for spiritual understanding

Hunter - Birth through High School

Collage of Hunter Nathanael Smith and Carol Crawford Smith
Photos taken September 1993 – June 2011

SCENE 6

Angel among Us

God is with us always and was there the day he was born. His name is Emmanuel.

THOUGHTS AND MEMORIES OF MY children forever flow in my spirit and remain etched on my mind. The legacy my second born son built is one that I believe only a person of divine providence could create: "I see Jesus over there." Between bites of a jelly doughnut, Garland uttered these majestic words with calm assurance. We were in the Carol Lee doughnut shop twisting on diner-style red, round-cushioned pedestal seats. The view out the window in front of us was straight at the Henderson Lawn hill on the Virginia Tech campus. On that beautiful clear day, my baby paused to tell me who he saw. Garland was three years young and knew of Jesus through Bible lessons and church service scripture readings and sermons. I always sensed his profound connection to the Divine. I saw it for the first time through the clear plastic bed when he was a newborn, lying naked with patches and cords from a monitor attached to his chest. The equipment was necessary because Garland came out the birth canal barely breathing. He did not make a sound, for his throat was filled with meconium. As soon as the umbilical cord was cut, the doctor and nurses hurriedly sucked the pea-green-colored waste out of his throat with rubber suction bulbs, then wrapped the baby up in a blanket and rushed him out of the delivery room.

After they checked my vitals to make sure I was okay, I was allowed to go to see Garland. He looked so feeble, yet angelic and peaceful, lying bare-bodied on his back in the plastic heated bed. His head was turned to his right side, and his eyes were closed. His chest expanded and contracted evenly to the rhythm of his breath. The monitor blinked happy smiling hearts—a reassuring sight, indicating he was doing fine. With each delicate breath he took, there was no doubt he was being watched over and blessed to live on. I wanted to hold him, to touch, rub, and caress his soft skin and kiss his tender forehead, but I could not yet because he needed to be monitored for an hour more. I stayed awhile to watch Garland breathe before returning to my maternity ward room to lie back down and wait for the nurse to bring him to me. When I finally held Garland in my arms, we connected instantly. What I saw then, when I was thirty-three years young, holds true and increases to this day: His spirit exudes the peace of one all-knowing. His loving demeanor is confident, caring, and forever-growing.

I believe Garland is an earth angel who intuitively knows exactly what to do and say at all times. In the early days of the diagnosis, when multiple sclerosis symptoms consumed my body and I had great difficulty walking, I would lie down often throughout the day. The guest bedroom was most convenient for resting because it was near the kitchen and the spare bathroom. One day when I was resting there, Garland came into the room and began rubbing my legs. I was sad and questioned why the disease was happening to me. As he rubbed my legs, Garland assured me calmly, "Don't worry, Mommy. It will all be over soon"—he was about four years young then. As Garland spoke, I knew God was speaking through him and guiding him as to exactly what to say. He confidently delivered his consolation as if my discomfort was no big deal. He was sure that what I was feeling would soon vanish like waves washed ashore erase inscriptions in beach sand. POOF—miraculously, the thought would be gone.

Hat Trick

Garland grew to be a talented soccer player who, on the soccer field, ran like a graceful gazelle gliding across an African terrain, ready to take flight with eagles. If you know soccer, you know that a hat trick is when a player scores three goals in one game. Garland has done that many times since he began playing soccer as a little boy, and he has always scored at least three in one in the field of my heart. Three is a definitive number. There is the Holy Trinity in Christianity: the Father, the Son, the Holy Spirit, which is very real to me. In the game of baseball, there are three strikes, and you're out. There is Tic-Tac-Toe—which you can play on paper, in the sand, on the sidewalk with chalk or wherever and however creative you can make it—where three Xs or three Os, lined up vertically, horizontally, or diagonally after alternating turns with an opponent, results in a win.

We know these truths. We know the games. But, how do you explain a birth at 3:33 PM on the twenty-seventh of the twelfth month (twelve days after the due date of the fifteenth) when I was thirty-three years young, with all numbers divisible by three? Three-thirty-three, twenty-seven, twelve, fifteen, and thirty-three have the commonality of being divisible by three, which has me convinced Garland is an angel of God born in the name of the Father, the Son, and the Holy Spirit, able to produce hat tricks with effortless ease.

I cannot express enough how grateful I am for Garland. He was there for me in ways greater than anyone else could be or would. Garland never refused to help me, though I know he struggled on an emotional level as well as on a physical level. He had to watch his mother deteriorate physically, with no one to talk to or take council with about these events and how they were affecting him. With his father gone from my life and regularly from his life, Garland, with his brother, handled the responsibility of helping me. Then, once Hunter went to college and passed, the task of caregiving fell greatly on Garland. When Garland was strong enough, he lifted me in and out of the bed. When he was old enough, he drove me where I needed to go. It was not fair to him to be expected to be my caregiver. Though a part of me wanted to believe he was superhuman and could take care of me, the reality was that he was a kid, growing, discovering, and learning to survive in life. As he grew older, circumstances with Garland frequently occurred to remind me he was a child and, in fact, human. Life turned out to be filled with the exact experiences necessary for me to be able to revere Garland's humanness and for him to freely live, learn, survive, and soar in confidence.

Building Wings

My perfect angel Garland proved time and again that he was human, as he greatly desired fine quality items found in the material world. Ever since Garland was a little boy, his great needs and desires were backed by very expensive taste. It did not surprise me that he had expectations for the best money could buy. I was the same when I was a kid, and the apple that was Garland did not fall far from the tree. Besides, I impressed upon him at a very early age that when you do and give your best, you deserve the best in return. My thinking was more metaphoric, but his understanding always fell in the realm of the literal.

For example, as soon as Garland was old enough to know the distinction, he wanted the most durable soccer ball and cleats, which always seemed to be the most expensive. I wanted my son to have the items, believing such possessions would lead to his happiness. I would buy him whatever he wanted, even at times when money was tight. It was my way of making up for him not having a father around and of helping to fill the void. Buying him what he asked for was also my way of thanking him for helping me, especially when he got older. I knew better than to think possessions could buy happiness and express complete gratitude, but I thought that way on some level for a while. My acquiescing to Garland's impulsive and big-ticket desires clearly perpetuated his demands. He knew that if he asked, I would provide as best I could. I also encouraged him to practice the art of Ask-Believe-Receive: One must ask for exactly what is desired, believe the desire will become a reality, and then be ready to receive the desire. For those reasons, I could not blame him for expecting and insisting on receiving the best.

In addition to soccer, Garland loved "board" sports, and he received the best for that activity as well. Skateboarding was his favorite pastime during the spring, summer and fall when he was not kicking balls and scoring on the soccer field. Garland would go to the town skate park and spend hours grinding above rails and flying over sets of stairs with the board connected or hovering close underfoot. In winter, on days off from school, when snow was plentiful and the only place to play soccer was indoors at the recreation center, Garland was gliding down the snow-covered hills at the nearby golf course on a 350-dollar snowboard—which I bought for him—looking just as peaceful and at ease as a marine sailing along the deep blue waters while standing on an ocean liner deck. Yes, Garland lived the good life he well deserved. And I had provided that life as best I could.

God's Beauty

More than buying Garland things, I saw enjoying the delights of our natural surroundings as a remedy for what he may have felt was missing or lacking. The magnificence of each season is what I could affordably and satisfyingly turn to year-round for my, Garland, and also Hunter's peace of mind and contentment during their adolescent years. Fall meant bright sunflowers, sweet grapes and many-colored leaves for me. During that season we would ride the Blue Ridge Parkway, which was about forty minutes from our home, and experience a landscape of rich gold, bronze, and copper-hued foliage. It was a time to witness "God's Beauty" and its splendid palette.

God's Beauty—a name I coined—is a mountainous-valley-view just a hop, skip, and a jump from my front door. I came upon it on a drive searching for a house, long before finding my property. I would frequent the top of a neighborhood hill to see the breathtaking mountainous sight of foliage down and out in Ellett Valley. It was a place I'd often take Hunter and Garland to experience year-round in times past, when they were little and I was physically able to drive. I wanted my sons to feel the amazement I felt and recognize the magnificence of our region—a beauty so magnificent and available practically at our doorstep.

In winter, colors were browns and grays covering the earth of barren-twigged trees sprouted on a balding mountain "dandruff-filled" with fresh white snow. Spring offered a delicious vision of vibrant lime, lemon grass, and bok choy greens with sprays of lavender-colored rose buds here and there to visually delight hungry eyes and minds. Come summer, I wanted to reach, touch, and comb my fingers through the trees thick with lush green leaves and pick through tangled briar-brush patches, to graciously leave it a manicured assemblage of nature-produced growth.

The sight of God's Beauty during autumn warmed my heart and made me feel safe and secure. I knew, upon seeing the grandeur of the changing leaves, that life for me would release what was dying and dead and no longer serving me and set the stage for revival and fresh awareness. I found joy in the warm and brilliant colors and refreshing scents of the fall season. These things reminded me I had functioning eyes to see and perfect nasal faculties to smell. I found happiness on a quiet, cool fall morning, enjoying God's Beauty with the simple joy of biting a crisp apple. My salivary glands awakened as the chewed fruit spread over my tongue and passed smoothly down my throat through my digestive tract. I was completely happy and alive right then and there within nature's stage, which was set for rebirth.

The sight of God's beauty and all its splendid sensory gifts was a delightful attraction that I returned to year-round to deflect the trials that came with my conscious and uncompromising determination to raise Hunter and Garland as a single mother. Raising my sons and establishing a sense of stability and permanence was a success. I would reap that success with the support of family and friends, but in the end I was the primary parent, responsible for providing the accomplishment. In accepting my responsibility and achievement, God's Beauty in all its perfection reminded me of how perfectly the world is ordered and how perfectly I was made. Included in that perfection was how I performed as a mother. It was important for me to connect strongly with Garland on a non-material level. As is human nature, Garland gravitated to possessions, yet he showed great love and sensitivity for nature. I especially loved the just-described quality of his humanness. Perhaps the frequent parkway drives and careening over God's beauty sharpened his taste for the splendid richness of nature. Those were the desires and characteristics I would help him capitalize on and make advantageous for his optimal personal, athletic, and academic development. Garland was a strong student academically while in high school, with a healthy athletic physique and an admirably healthy self-esteem on top of it all. The former two strengths were enriched by him being grade-conscious, like Hunter, and engaging in sports and outdoor activities year-round, the latter of which was enhanced by a popularity factor. As a high-school junior, Garland ran for senior class president and won the seat and the privileges that came with it. I was so proud of him when he spoke as an officer at his graduation from Blacksburg High School in May of 2013. Once Garland was no longer in high school proper, he would continue to represent the school as a member of the soccer team. The team had a very successful season and made it to the final top-two teams in its division and earned a chance at the VHSL state championship in early-June after Garland graduated.

I was even more happy, proud, and excited for Garland. He would play for the second time in an AA Division high-school soccer championship game. The first was played his freshman year, and they had won the state title. Now a graduated senior and as a soccer team captain, he better understood the significance of qualifying for a high-school soccer championship game, and he did not take the accomplishment lightly. Garland was now one of the guys the other team members looked up to and respected. He was a team captain, accepting responsibility for the actions of his teammates; he was charged with deciding disciplinary measures for teammates, when necessary, and with giving accolades as well. Garland's healthy self-esteem and good sense were developed through years of his giving and doing the best he could and receiving the best I could provide. Garland's goodness also developed from his being raised with my maternal influence to appreciate the divine gifts of body and nature that are generously bestowed upon us and this world. In the end, Garland was raised and positioned to lead and love in a divine, non-material way.

Garland recognized my influence and acknowledged that I was always there for him, through thick and thin, as he had experienced through the years. Before the high-school soccer championship game, during a turning-point conversation, Garland told me, with tears in his eyes and riveting emotion in his voice, that I was his heart and that he loved me dearly. Garland was a man of few words, and for him to express himself in such a way was like hearing my son recite a short story. Always insightful and always thoughtful in his words, Garland would express himself infrequently, and when he did, it was with truth, great wisdom, and included direct eye contact. I knew, with that conversation, that my angel was as strong, as loving, and as confident as ever. He was not at all tainted from years of me buying him what he wanted. I saw his vibrant spirit become even brighter through the tears he shed and the words he spoke of loving me forevermore, just days before his impending championship soccer game.

Championship Soccer Game

Saturday, June 8, 2013 was the day of the Virginia High School League AA Division Men's Soccer Championship game. I very much wanted the Bruins to win the state title, and I felt blessed to be there to witness the game. A win would mark the team's twelfth state title. That number of victories for a single high school team was unprecedented. The two high school teams that had come closest won six titles each. It would mean so much to Garland and his teammates to go home with the trophy. They worked so hard and with great athleticism all season to end it undefeated, and they greatly wanted and deserved the championship. It was time to cap off Garland's high school soccer career with a monumental victory.

Parents and fans collected in the stands, and news photographers and videographers were positioned on the field and in the press box. Starters for both teams, one of whom was Garland, and referees stood at attention center field for introductions. Spectators quieted and stood still during the canned music of the "Star Spangled Banner" screeching through the intercom. Yes, we were free people that championship game day and living in a free nation; however, in that focused moment of celebrating our freedom in song, I reflected and thought about the European settlers who had come to America in search of a better life, devoid of dictatorship. These settlers would then take free ways of living from the indigenous dwellers, capture and import humans across the middle passage, and create a history of enslavement in this country. Though uncomfortable with the past, I could not change it, so I became presently grateful my son was free and in position to play, and that I was alive and there to see it.

The thought was cut short when applause began after the National Anthem, and the team gathered on the field in their motivation huddle. The BHS Bruins team shouted their "power roar"—named here for the purpose of this writing, as they said something different at the end of each huddle, according to Garland—then immediately positioned center field for the start whistle.

Our defense gained and kept control of the ball early. Seven minutes into the game, the Bruins were up 2–0 and held the lead into the second half. As a forward, Garland was used to scoring, and he was determined to get a goal in this final game. Each time he got the ball, he maneuvered and dribbled it around and between opponents straight to the goal to shoot when there was a clear opportunity. His first kick at the goal was a point-blank shot straight into the goalkeeper's chest and arms, leaving no chance of scoring. His second attempt went over the keeper's head, grazing the keeper's glove-covered fingertips as he jumped to stop the ball. The keeper did not stop the ball that time, though. It zipped over his head, straight for the net, but it soared a tad too high and rebounded off the cross bar.

Tears flowed down Garland's face the entire second half of the game. Not because he had not gotten a goal yet, but because he knew his team being up 2–0 meant a probable win. The Bruins' defense was relentless. They controlled the ball constantly and quickly reclaimed possession whenever it was lost. Thirty-five minutes into the second half, the ball was kicked out of bounds by an opponent. We threw it back in straight for a sure one-two combination to score. The thrown-in ball bounced to #17, Williams, who made a powerful and high—at least thirty feet—kick straight to #10, Smith. The ball did not even touch the ground. Garland jumped and made contact with it in the air and headed it straight into the back left corner of the net.

The crowd jumped and cheered! The tears were really flowing then as Garland turned and ran in victory, extending his arms like wings in flight. If he had flying powers, surely he would have taken off. A divine force had taken hold of Garland at that moment and enlivened my angel, fully strengthening his wings.

I had never felt anything more beautiful for my son than what I felt at that moment. I felt his peace and relief for the accomplished goal, and I felt peace within myself for our trying and ultimately successful voyage through our game of life, in which I provided the best in raising Garland. That was behind us at that victorious moment. In the game of soccer, Garland had just scored the third and final goal of the high school league championship game, sealing the win at 3–0 for the AA Division Virginia state soccer championship title. He was so overcome with emotion at that point.

A newspaper photographer captured a very moving image of the victory sprint Garland took immediately after the final header goal. His tears do not show in the picture for him running so fast, but they were there. That moment was highly emotional, not just for him but for me and others as well. If a photographer had snapped pictures of the parents in the stands, there would be many more images of faces full of relieved tears at the joyful victory. The header goal made by Garland was the final goal of the game, the final goal of the season, and his final goal as a soccer player with the entire Blacksburg High School team. It was a very poetic ending to a glorious high school life and a victorious high school soccer career.

Collage of Garland Thomas-Emmanuel Smith and Carol Crawford Smith
Photos taken January 1996 – June 2013

SCENE 7

Boys to Men

"The love I have for them is unconditional, as a mother's love should be. I may have fallen short in some ways—what parent hasn't?—but I did better than the best I could do, which is everything!"

My beautiful Hunter's person and needs were never once neglected during Garland's high school triumphs. As he grew and entered early-adulthood, I only knew what to address with Hunter if and when he opened up to me. Hunter's transition into being more confident and autonomous occurred long after he had graduated from high school, when he was an upper classmen in college. Hunter was a gorgeous, phenomenal human being with love for himself and others and, to my great advantage, benefit, and blessing, love for me.

I benefitted tremendously from Garland's love, as well. Garland was, and will always be, my angel. I still believe he is an old soul, led by a divine force to do what is right and good. Garland was like my therapist at times. I found comfort in speaking to him about whatever was troubling or of wonder to me. Once he matured to a young man, he offered thought-filled advice and suggestions with the wisdom of a sage.

There is a spiritual beauty, as well as an intimidating possibility, in my description of Garland as a sage-confidante. What if he knew more than me, and he chose me to be his mother prior to conception because his spirit knew he could help me, peacefully and successfully, through this life and because, from past life association, he knew me better than I know myself? I do not expect anyone to understand the aforesaid statement or have an answer for the question. I am grappling with the concept myself and only ask that the idea be pondered—I put the thought out there because it flashed in my mind. Just like the notion occurred in my life's journey that I possess a powerful and potent ability to raise human beings, namely Hunter and Garland.

Humor me briefly as I attempt to be funny and render a scenario of my life as a mother: "Oh, if only I could bottle up and market the steps taken and years lived to raise my sons and help them reach their known stage in life. I'd be a multi-billionaire, and the world would be a more focused, loving, and generous place, if the product, once bought, was applied to create more human beings like Hunter and Garland. There would be no greed because children like Garland would generously spend and share with others using their mother's debit card and hard-earned cash. There would be no lack or need for the same reason and also because, like Hunter, people would not want anything except the bare minimum. There would be no selfishness—except for when one child messes with his or her sibling's stuff. The world would only have to buy the formula and take it to realize the perfect state of family, like the one I created on the blank canvas in my mind with ideally desirable imagery."

The start of the composition of the ideal image was a mother and child. Though I knew I could be content as a single mother and felt confident that a child was all I needed to be happy, I diverted my focus, and the husband became part of the picture after I convinced myself I could paint a pleasing composition with the husband included. The husband and I were incompatible, though. My error was in thinking I could change him, as if instantly changing my artistic strength from painting to sculpting, and mold and polish him into an image that I desired, to be admired and cherished. If I had approached the relationship with the sensibilities of a painter—the medium that metaphorically resonates with me best—I would have seen that the colors or spirits clashed.

My mistake was not to hold out for the right material (man) or complementary colors (personality) to complete the composition of marriage and family as I had originally envisioned fitting me best. Still, Chester was my husband, and he is my children's father. For them he was the right father and, in the end, that's what's important. Chester was not a bad person. He was simply not right for me. It was not possible for me to change to understand him, to relate to him or to coordinate with his way of thinking and being. My sons were able to see his divinity, his human-ness, though they knew him as flawed, and they saw that in me, too. I also acknowledge the divinity within Chester. I acknowledge that Chester and I, through divine ordination, gave the world Hunter and Garland, and for that, and for Chester, I am eternally grateful. I forgive Chester, and myself too, for once seeing differently and for our family life not working out as we thought it should.

There is much that remains unknown to me about Chester regarding our children. I reflect and wonder if he saw what I saw when our sons were born. We never discussed such meaningful observations when together. I saw Garland as an all-knowing and generous human being from the very beginning, and I thought Hunter was the most beautiful baby I had ever seen. At birth, Hunter had a head full of fine, black hair covering his entire head and a fair complexion with rosy cheeks blushed from being newly touched by the air and from producing his first cry. When calm, his tender lips would purse and motion as if he'd been sipping on the amniotic fluid in my womb and needed something else to suck, which would almost immediately be the nipple of my breast to extract milk. From the way he latched on with a strong grip, then drew and pulled the fluid, it was clear he was an intuitively determined human being who knew how to get what he needed and wanted to live. Oh my God, I was so in love with that new person born of me!

I admired Hunter for committing to finding the person he became and resisting the incongruous influence and stifling opinions of others in the process. So long as Hunter was not knowingly hurting himself or anyone, he conducted himself confidently and truthfully for his happiness. I learned from Hunter that is how I must live and be as well.

Garland, as I expected and hoped, grew to be a sincere, trustworthy, and self-assured man. When it became too much for him and his health to help me, he let me know as politely and as efficiently as possible. When I called and asked for his help "just one last time," he texted me the reply "I wish you wouldn't still ask me to do these things," and then "I'm exhausted and need to go straight to Radford to sleep." Garland had matriculated at Radford University—about thirty minutes from Blacksburg—in the fall of 2013. He was recruited to play on the D1 Highlanders Men's Soccer team.

During the summer before his junior year at Radford University, Garland worked as a night auditor at an inn in downtown Blacksburg. Like my childhood sweetheart, Aaron, Garland worked nocturnally, from midnight to eight o'clock, and slept most of the day. To ask him to help me out of bed one more time in the morning after work was a request he could not fulfill. When he politely texted me "Can you please just wait for your helper?" I knew the time had long past for me to let go and stop depending on Garland. His reply was kind and simple, and I understood clearly.

Garland had taken a necessary self-imposed break from helping me. It was past time for me to no longer rely exclusively on him. I had to let my guard down and call on others for help. He had to be free to live and grow beyond me, and the time had come for me to reflect and grow, for me.

FINALE

Me, Myself, and I

"So there I sat, a proud parent, a free and independent woman, and a person alone, realizing that the only one I should depend on is me. It took a half-century for me to claim the thought that next to God I am number one always, to articulate the words, to really mean it, and to follow through."

ONCE I READ IT, I use to think my life was similar to that of the heroine in *The Notebook,* where girl meets boy at a tender young age and falls in like, then love, to explore and experience what males and females are drawn to do, as was the case for Aaron and me. Later in life, young woman ignites love with a man and discovers a more mature love, in a pure sexual sense, that is beyond romantic and absolutely beautiful. Their adult love is indescribable and best equates to spiritual ecstasy. That was the love phenomenon of Bennett and me. Time passes, and the desire to achieve life's milestones arises, so the adult friends and lovers break up, but stay in touch through the decades where marriage, children, divorce, and illness—human stuff—happens. That is <u>A</u>aron, <u>B</u>ennett, <u>C</u>hester, <u>D</u>is-ease—multiple sclerosis—and me intertwined in the ménage of my life—the ABCs of my life. So there I sat, a proud parent, a free and independent woman, and a person alone, realizing that the only one I should depend on is me. It took a half- century for me to claim the thought that next to God I am number one always, to articulate the words, to really mean it, and to follow through.

I am now fifty-one. I am very excited about this age as it means I have lived gloriously through the first half of my life—assuming I live to be at least 102 years young, as desired. It is the beginning of the rest of my life. I have clarity now like never before. My focus is on me and taking care of me first. I am no longer a victim of the world mind. I no longer feel responsible for others and their happiness. That includes my parents and my sons. And, there is no man in my life for doting on, caring for, and supporting—which is both relieving and sad at the same time, for I do want to be with a special someone. My focus is on me and the moment, and I have a great sense of relief! I am relieved to be free and to know I can explore me. I am always listening and attentive to where I am drawn and need to be for me.

A significant moment of my latest self-actualization occurred the winter before Hunter passed. He was in the kitchen cooking with his friend from high school, Britney, and Garland had just walked in the door with his long-time friend, Johanna. It was winter break, and both sons are home from college. The joyful season was filled with a beautiful spirit of love and sex…Yes, sex! I was not having any, but I was sure feeling and thinking about it more, than I had in a long time. My libido was reawakening mentally and physically. I had beautiful, innocent dreams of sharing love. One night I dreamt that my bus driver, Irvin, came searching for me after I had hinted wanting to be intimate with him. I wasn't sure at the time if he got the hint, but his looking for me in my dream cleared the doubt.

Irvin and I went to a hotel in my dream. It was plain and unimpressive but clean, just like Irvin. The bed was made with a cover like my grandmother had owned and my mother found plentifully in thrift shops and five-and-dime stores for a dollar. It was pink and white, with a bumpy floral-relief surface that was definitely not my taste but charming and reminiscent of family. I felt comfortable sharing love in such surroundings with

Irvin, whom I barely knew. The sole purpose of being intimate with Irvin was to ignite the fire within me that had stopped roaring. I had not shared love with a man in years. I missed the warmth of sexual intimacy with another human being. In my dream with Irvin, however, sex was calculated, clean, orderly, and boring. As sex-starved as I was, I was happy to have awakened from the Stepford Wives-like unconsciousness with Irvin, and happy and at peace realizing, accepting, admitting, and sharing that I am a beautiful, sexual human being, and there is everything right with that. God made me, made humans with sex organs and sexual parts so we can know pleasure and ecstasy beyond this physical realm, but in a spiritual realm, which is where I believe as humans, we must strive to reach, in order to return from whence we came. I have come near to reaching that state in body, mind, and spirit in this lifetime, but for the past two decades, no love sharing experience has come close to the exhilarating, sexually satisfying times Bennett and I had shared and none equaled what I once hoped to have with Aaron, nor has any come close to the love I share with my audience and self when dancing. Yes, dance for me is a love-sharing experience.

Sons and Love

I can talk on and on about my experiences and thoughts on men and love-sharing, but the memories I have pale in comparison to the triumphs and trials of life with my beautiful sons. The six months with Garland after the state championship victory were full of more occurrences that left me both proud and reflecting. He was named to the all-star team for our region of the state. He scored a single goal for his team at that game and was named Most Valuable Player.

I recall the earliest memories of innocence and calm to keep me in awe of Garland. When he said, "I see Jesus over there" between bites of his jelly doughnut, I just wanted to kiss, hug, and hold him in all his precious sweetness. I had never heard nor seen anything more beautiful. I felt so honored and blessed to be in his presence and to hear him speak of witnessing such divinity. Yes, my child and I were twisting on round, red pedestal diner seats in the doughnut shop, but we could have easily been in Jerusalem on Via de la Rosa on the day Christ carried the Cross to Mount Calvary. Garland's words were so calm, assuring, and convincing. I was at great peace at that moment with Garland and grateful to Chester for agreeing that we should go to church as a family when the boys were young. At that reflective moment, I realized the years spent with Chester were not worthless nor in vain. I inwardly thanked Chester. Our union produced two wonderful children, one of which, I was reminded that day, had a profound connection to God. My message to Garland for his eighteenth birthday incorporated that divine donut shop story. I posted it on Facebook and entitled it, "Angel Among Us." The opening statement read "God is with us always and was there the day he was born. His name is Garland Thomas-Emmanuel (Emmanuel meaning 'God is with us'), and today is his eighteenth birthday." Garland is an absolute blessing, an angel in the guise of a man. My sweet angel is God's perfection, and I love him more than words can express.

Almost three months earlier when Hunter turned twenty, I shared these sentiments: "Twenty years ago, the most beautiful baby boy I had ever seen, with spirit-filled eyes and a head full of jet-black hair, was laid upon my chest for me to hold in my arms. At that moment he was named Hunter Nathanael and became known to me as 'One', with the middle name Nathanael meaning 'Gift of God.' Upon seeing and holding Hunter, I felt eternal gratitude for the gift of him that was forever mine… I thank God for twenty years of love, life, laughter, and learning with my baby-turned-young-man."

Hunter was truly a blessing in my life and in this world. I looked forward to ever more of those four 'Ls' with Hunter. From our time together as Carol Crawford Smith and Hunter Nathanael Smith, I have lasting fond memories of our days gone by. In addition to his plethora of talents and abilities, Hunter was an exceptional writer, and I treasure many of the special stories he wrote as an adolescent.

Growing Beans
By
Hunter Smith

I would say my favorite science experiment was when my 4th grade class planted beans. The materials were a bean, a cup, tissue, and water.

The first day we did the experiment we put the bean in the tissue and put the tissue in the cup. Then we put a few drops of water on the tissue and put it on the windowsill. The class had to write about how the beans were growing. I saw some little roots coming from the bean. I couldn't believe it was growing without soil. In about two more weeks the beans were ready to be taken home. That experiment was awesome.

True to form, what is done for one son, I do for the other, so here I share the cutest story written by Garland that he claims I made him write in third grade.

A Better Community
By
Garland Smith

A better community takes a lot of hard work, money, and responsibility to change it or to fix it. For example, you could put tons of trampolines all over town so you could hop to work every day and play soccer on trampolines every day. So, you would basically do everything on trampolines though that would be a big waist. That's why we do small adjustments to the community. For example, put small community businesses or shops next to Kroger or a place like that and shop there instead.

A good change is to make a new type of car that is smaller and that doesn't run on fuel, but uses water or something like that to run on. Or, make a new house on the street and ask other people to pitch in on the act, so it wouldn't cost as much as to hire someone to do it for you.

Everyone could have a robot to do all of their chores like walk the dog, do the dishes, and clean up messes, etc. The robots would do everything for us while we lounge on the couch watching TV like we did before we created adults. They were for work only. But then one day Father decided not to do any work and turned away. Soon all the adults turned away and created an army and drove the BND (Boys Next Door) away, cut down the ULTRA SUPER MEGA TRIPLE TREEHOUSE, and blasted away in a rocket to the moon. Soon the adults wanted the boys back so they went to the moon base and got two boys and brought them back home and made small groupings called families.

As you read in the previous paragraph, that all meant that before adults, we children could do whatever we wanted, whenever we wanted, and where ever we wanted. Trying not to get off the subject, here's the next paragraph.

Another good change is to make prices go down at the restaurants and gas stations everywhere, so you save money and don't spend as much. The savings could go in the bank for particular reasons like buying food, buying clothes, and buying toys for your son or daughter.

Those are a lot, and a lot, and a lot of reasons to help make your community better. But, more is coming. Just a few more words left to finish the report.

As I was saying, you could make a capsule that you throw to make an instant campsite, fire, shelter, technology, etc. That would change the community because everything would be taken care of in a snap.

There are over 200 words now. My mom made me do this, and I'm finally DONE!!!

I am in stiches reading these stories! My life was complete with Hunter and Garland, no matter how hard I tried to twist it, think, and state differently. They were gorgeous, hilarious and brilliant. They were the special ingredients in the formula that made life worth waking up to every morning and reinforce the class act that I am.

Carol Crawford Smith Family
Portrait, August 2008

Here completes a disclosure of my life, what I do, and what I have done, which I reiterate is synonymous with give, take, be. Unconditional love and endless sacrifice for my children is one way I give. Living a sensible, true, and honest existence, indiscriminately and fairly evaluating life circumstances to determine and decide how best to address them, for me is to take. All said, I am a lover who loves deeply and dearly. As a youth, I knew love for a person outside of family. As an adult, I learned how to be loved and how to create the greatest loves of my life, my sons. Intertwined within this amorous existence is my life-sustaining love for dance that shapes my path and conversations. Mother, love, and dance are the trinity of ingredients which, when mixed together with uncompromising poise and grace, formulate the one and only me, I know to be.

Give Take Be is a memoir that selectively brushes the surface of the life of Carol Crawford Smith. It is a snapshot of three phases or acts, if you will, of my life, which has so much more living, loving, and laughing remaining. I must laugh to tears some more, like I do when watching the hilarious out takes of the Carol Burnette Show (1967–1978). I must laugh to tears some more like I do to this day when cracking up with my DTH girlfriends at the "Jam, Jelly, Toast" inside joke. I must laugh to tears some more like I do when watching clips of today's youth analyze a photo of Steven Spielberg sitting in front of a "dead" Triceratops dinosaur on the set of Jurassic Park and hearing the youth call the director despicable and inhumane. Some observers thought it was a rhinoceros and Spielberg, 'the hunter,' had killed it and was posing for a picture in front of his game—Truthfully, I did not know whether to laugh or cry when watching that clip, as the critics/commentators were the generation of our future.

My continued living includes watching more enjoyable movies like *Best Man Holiday* (2014), *Pride and Prejudice* (2005), *The Notebook* (2004), and *Turning Point* (1977) over and over and over again. These are the kinds of films that bring me joy and happiness when I watch them. For me, life can always include more of such good things.

Love for my children, love for my family, and my love for dance is forever. Love, as far as my relationships are concerned, were my choice to go into and to get out of. Obviously, it was not meant for me to be with the lovers in my life to date throughout my lifetime and for a lifetime. After all, if the relationships were meant to last until my dying day, I'd still be in one of them, right? I ask this question at the risk of sounding pathetic, yet knowing I am a person to be heralded, emulated, respected, and loved for that is what I reciprocate.

Thank you for reading this *Give Take Be* journey of my existence. I am so grateful you took the time to care and to learn more. In closing, I have a request: Give of you to others freely and abundantly; Take and sift through the wisdom received in life to find gems, and share them unselfishly; Be in this world exactly what you were created for, as it is a gift bestowed upon you to benefit humanity in return.

Stage Black

LIGHTS UP

Bows

- *Aaron is gone but not forgotten.*
- *Bennett is married with children and still makes music.*
- *Chester is a respected father of Hunter and Garland.*
- *Hunter and Garland are my great loves.*
- *I live in an extreme house with flowers (no boxes) out front.*
- *I love my life!*

ENCORE

Dance is a Love in My Life

"Never say 'never'; Inspired by Woodson."

Exhausted, sweating profusely, and boogieing my butt off
It's the late 1960s.
James Brown sings *I Got the Feelin', Papa's Gotta Brand New Bag, Hot Pants, Cold Sweat*
Kids cheer
Do the Split!
Do the Split!
Do the Split!
I do a full split at age seven.
I end every dance at every birthday party with a split.
On the living room dance floor,
I show off the best funky chicken, skate, kick-ball-change.
I love the attention and accolades from peer teeny boppers.
I love the attention so much!
I dance from the beginning
To the end of the music played.
I show off my wiggly-worm and jerk moves like no other.
Everybody loves me.
I love being loved for my dancing, as much as I love to dance.

Dancing is so freeing.
Dancing is exhilarating!
I dance for hours, perspiring.
Shuffle to the fruit punch table.
Take a quick thirst-quenching swallow from a Dixie cup.
Camel back
Pony Hop-Swim
Dance is a love in my life.

Carol Crawford Smith, May 1995

CURTAIN CLOSED

Ghost Lights

Afterword

Barbara Pendergrass, Ed.D.
Dean Emerita of Students, Virginia Tech

I THINK AN APPROPRIATE SUBTITLE for this book is "The Men I Have Loved and Who Have Loved Me." From childhood love with Aaron to adult love with Bennett and Chester, her vivid descriptions help the characters to become real to the readers. Carol and Aaron gave childhood love a new dimension. Their deep passion and commitment to the well-being of each other was evident throughout their relationship. One can only read and hope for a happy ending to this everlasting love story. Although Bennett and Chester were significant relationships, Aaron is the most memorable of the personalities. Carol's images of her love for her sons, (Hunter and Garland) and her father provide a vivid picture of what unconditional love looks and feels like.

Carol Crawford Smith demonstrates her courage and integrity in telling her truths. The details of her life present a picture of a person with a ravenous thirst for living, loving, being loved, and giving. The title "Give Take Be," a familiar term to ballet dancers, is given a new meaning in the book. As Carol paints a portrait of her life, one experiences her giving spirit

– her willingness to give her time, share her talents, and most importantly, her willingness to give and share her love.

I equate the "take" with her willingness to take risks. As a teenager, she left home to live in an apartment alone to pursue her passion, dancing. She demonstrates a profound maturity and sense of self at an early age. Readers, especially young readers will gain courage and strength from her story.

The book ends in the "be" stage. The passion is still there and her journey is not over. She makes no apology for being who she is. She has had many ups and downs. The diagnosis of MS, a painful divorce, and the death of her beloved son, Hunter would probably have rendered the average person powerless. But Carol is not an ordinary person. She is a strong super-gifted woman who continues to persevere through the various storms in her life. She will be! As I read her story, I could not help but think about the popular gospel song "I Won't Complain." Carol is thankful for the life she has lived and looks forward to the second phase of her life. While she has had some disappointments along the way, she relishes her many accomplishments, places visited, and people that she has met along her life journey.

I Won't Complain

I've had some good days. I've had some hills to climb. I've had some weary days. I've had some sleepless nights. But when I look around, and I think things over, all of my good days outweigh my bad days. So, I won't complain.

Acknowledgements

THERE ARE SO MANY PEOPLE in my life that I must thank for their influence that has led me to write this book. In addition to those named, pseudo-named and implied in the writing, I specifically thank my parents, Thomas and Elizabeth Crawford. It is because of them that I exist and have been allowed to actualize my plethora of creativity. I also choose to thank my children, Hunter and Garland. They inspire me every day to be the best I can be. I then choose to thank my Dance Theatre of Harlem family, especially Arthur Mitchell, Karel Shook and Shirley Mills. These directors believed in me as a young dancer and it is because of their belief that I developed an even greater belief in myself. An entire world of priceless life-lessons and opportunities opened onto me at their invitation. Embarking upon that world cast the mold for the strong and accomplished person I am. I am also enormously grateful for my Blacksburg, VA and greater community family. They have encouraged and supported me as a person, dance teacher and leader in the dance field since I graced the outstanding community. Because of their support, my dream to be an entrepreneur, dream home owner and beloved member of a society has come to fruition. Above all, I am grateful to God for the blessings bestowed upon me since before October 5, 1963, the day I was born.

Photo Details and Credits

- Refer to Act One; Lessons in Love; Scene One; Through the Classroom Window; Dance Theatre of Harlem and Living in New York City: Carol Crawford Smith standing before water in Dublin, Ireland; July 1979
- Refer to Act One; Lessons in Love; Scene One; Through the Classroom Window; Dance Theatre of Harlem and Living in New York City: Carol Crawford Smith sitting on bridge over the Po River in Turin, Italy; Photo taken by James Goree, July 1982
- Refer to Act One; Lessons in Love; Scene One; Through the Classroom Window; Dance Theatre of Harlem and Living in New York City: Carol Crawford Smith and Hugues Magen posing in front of DTH poster at Kennedy Center for the Performing Arts in Washington, D. C.; Photo taken by James Goree, February 1987
- Refer to Act One; Lessons in Love; Scene One; Through the Classroom Window; Dance Theatre of Harlem and Living in New York City: Carol Crawford Smith posing with Augustus van Heerden and Hugues Megan in the romantically playful pas de trois in the second movement of Billy Wilson's *Concerto in F*; Photo taken by Kris Craig for Providence (Rhode Island) Journal Bulletin, October 1987
- Refer to Act One; Lessons in Love; Scene One; Through the Classroom Window; Dance Theatre of Harlem and Living in New

York City: Carol Crawford Smith posing in front of the Kremlin in Moscow, Russia; Photo taken by James Goree, May 1988

- Refer to Act One; Lessons in Love; Scene Two; Bennett; The Proposal: Carol Crawford Smith and Family (Thomas Crawford, Dr. Charlene A. Peterson, Elizabeth Crawford) at Marymount Manhattan College graduation; *Photographer Unknown,* June 1991
- Refer to Act One; Lessons in Love; Scene Three; Specious; Path to Eternal Dancing: Dancers on Stage Rehearsing Doina at Herod's Theater in Caesarea, Israel; Photo taken by Carol Crawford Smith, June 1981
- Refer to Act One; Lessons in Love; Scene Three; Specious; Path to Eternal Dancing: Carol Crawford Smith as Princess of Unreal Beauty Performing in Firebird ballet with Charmaine Hunter, Melanie Person and Augustus van Heerden; *Photographer Unknown,* Photo taken 1987
- Refer to Act Two; Moving the Bus; Scene Four; Extreme Makeover; From Door Knock to Dream House: Carol Crawford Smith, Hunter Nathanael Smith, Garland Thomas-Emmanuel Smith with Ty Pennington; Photo taken by Deborah Travis, December 2005
- Refer to Act Two; Moving the Bus; Scene Four; Extreme Makeover; From Door Knock to Dream House: Building Specialists, Inc. Ad, December 2005
- Refer to Act Three; We Are Family; Scene Five; One; Surreal News: Hunter Nathanael Smith's UVA Diploma, Photo taken by Thomas Crawford, May 2015
- Refer to Act Three; We Are Family; Scene Five; One; Surreal News: Collage of Hunter Nathanael Smith and Carol Crawford Smith created by Carol Crawford Smith, Photos taken September 1993 – June 2011 by Carol Crawford Smith Family and Friends and Matt Gentry for Roanoke (Virginia) Times

- Refer to Act Three; We Are Family; Scene Six; Angel among Us; Championship Soccer Game: Collage of Garland Thomas-Emmanuel Smith and Carol Crawford Smith created by Carol Crawford Smith, Photos taken January 1996 – June 2013 by Carol Crawford Smith Family and Friends including Jay Williams and Matt Gentry for Roanoke (Virginia) Times

- Refer to Act Three; We Are Family; FINALE; Sons and Love: Carol Crawford Smith, Hunter Nathanael Smith and Garland Thomas-Emmanuel Smith Family, Portrait taken by Theresa M. Smerud, August 2008

- Refer to ENCORE; Dance is a Love in My Life: Carol Crawford Smith in dance pose; Photo taken by Gary Buss, May 1995

- Refer to About the Author: Carol Crawford Smith, Author; Photo taken by Michael Bolger

Additional thanks for Photo Details and Credits goes to:

Bob Fetzer of Building Specialist Inc., and Lorraine Graves, Charmaine Hunter, Hugues Magen, Melanie Person, Judy Tyrus, Augustus van Heerden, Theara J. Ward and Alexis “Holly” Wilson regarding certain Dance Theatre of Harlem images.

About the Author

CAROL CRAWFORD SMITH IS FOUNDER and artistic director of The Center of Dance in Blacksburg, Virginia (Established August 1994). Through her dance school she provides instruction, workshops, and programs of excellence in dance and related arts. Her professional experience in dance includes a ten-year career as a soloist with the internationally acclaimed Dance Theatre of Harlem (1978–1988).

Carol Crawford Smith has a Bachelor of Arts in Art History and Studio Art from Marymount Manhattan College (Graduated Magna Cum Laude as Carol Ann Crawford) and a Master of Science in Human Development with a concentration in Families and the Arts from Virginia Polytechnic Institute and State University (Virginia Tech). Crawford Smith has taught undergraduate courses at Marymount Manhattan College, the University of Hawaii–Hilo, and at Virginia Tech.

As a visual artist, Carol Crawford Smith creates CCDancer Designs ©; greeting cards and art featuring The Huelanders© - *People from the Land of Hue ©; A World of Color where People of All Colors Exist Harmoniously in One Colorful World ©.*

In December 2005, Carol Crawford Smith and her family were awarded a new home and renovated dance studio on ABC network's *Extreme Makeover: Home Edition.* The episode first aired February 12, 2006. In May 2006, she was a guest on the Montel Williams Show ("The Faces of MS" episode). Diagnosed with multiple sclerosis in 2000, Crawford Smith now candidly speaks and presents as a voice of inspiration and as an advocate to find a cure for the physically and cognitively debilitating disease that affects over five million people worldwide—usually in the prime of their lives. Crawford Smith used her voice and talent as a contributing writer to Mental Sharpening Stones by Jeffrey N. Gingold (July 2008; Demos Medical Publishing, New York, New York). In Chapter 6, 'The Dance of Life: Transformation to Maintaining Strength, Balance and Focus," Crawford Smith shares stories of her life as a single mother, world class dancer, and community leader and offers strategies and perspectives on how to maintain cognitive strength through her example of teaching dance and persevering with a positive attitude. Crawford Smith is also a columnist and contributor to *Dance Studio Life Magazine* (Gold Standard Press).

Carol Crawford Smith lives in Blacksburg, Virginia. Her website is <www.carolcrawfordsmith.com>. She welcomes correspondence at:

<Carol.Crawford.Smith.Writer@gmail.com>.